TWENTY-SECOND ANNUAL

1987

STEAM

PASSENGER SERVICE

DIRECTORY

**AN ILLUSTRATED DIRECTORY LISTING TOURIST
RAILROAD, TROLLEY AND MUSEUM OPERATIONS
WITH REGULARLY SCHEDULED OR INTERMITTENT
PASSENGER SERVICE.**

GUEST COUPONS

Be sure to use the reduced rate Guest Coupons included
in this Edition of the Steam Passenger Directory.

ISSN- 0081-542X

Empire State Railway Museum, Inc.
Middletown, New York

Stephen D. Bogen
Number 22

Marvin H. Cohen
1987 Edition

MARVIN H. COHEN
Editor

COVER PHOTO CREDITS

Front cover photograph courtesy Roaring Camp, Inc.
Roaring Camp & Big Trees Narrow-Gauge R.R.
train shown in the redwoods along the line.

Rear cover photograph by Marvin H. Cohen.
"Royal Hudson" No. 2860 prepares to back down
to its train at Squamish, British Columbia.

Published by the Empire State Railway Museum, Inc.
P.O. Box 666
Middletown, New York 10940
Phone (914) 343-4219

MEMBER

3

FOR YOUR INFORMATION

Listings
This Directory attempts to include every tourist railroad, trolley museum and railway museum in the United States and Canada about which reliable information can be secured. In order to be listed, railroads and other organizations must correspond directly with the Editors.

Accuracy
Every effort has been made to ensure the accuracy of the contents. The Editors, however, are totally dependent upon the information supplied by each individual listing. No responsibility can be assumed for errors, omissions, fare or schedule changes.

1988 Directory
To be published in May, 1988. New listings are welcome, space permitting. Deadline for information is March 1, 1988. For further information, contact the address shown below.

Brochures
Most railroads listed in this Directory offer free brochures and/or timetables except where specifically noted. Please enclose a large stamped, self-addressed envelope (SSAE).

Public Transportation
The Amtrak logo indicates scheduled rail passenger service to the city nearest the listed rail attraction. Railroad passenger service in effect at the time of publication and a reasonable distance from the site.

Advertising
Advertising space for the 1988 Directory may be reserved after January 1, 1988. When responding to advertisements in this issue, please mention the "Steam Directory". Your support will be appreciated.

Back Issues
Please see advertisement in rear of this Edition. The following issues are sold out: 1966, 1968, 1970, 1971 & 1985.

Railroads Not Listed
A few operating steam railroads are not shown in this Edition. Every effort has been made to obtain the necessary information and photographs, however, in a few cases a response has not been received. The Editors require a new response every year in order to be certain of the latest information.

Holidays
1987 U.S. Holidays referred to in this issue occur as follows: Memorial Day, May 25; Independence Day, July 4; Labor Day, September 7; Columbus Day, October 12; Thanksgiving Day, November 26; Christmas Day, December 25.

Comments
Comments and suggestions are welcomed and most are promptly answered. Persons with knowledge of new railway operations are encouraged to write, so that contact may be made for future editions.

Address all correspondence regarding the Steam Directory to:

Marvin H. Cohen, Editor
Empire State Railway Museum
P.O. Box 666
Middletown, New York 10940

9

COUNTRY TRAINS'
GIFTS FOR RAILROADERS

MORE THAN 150 + RAILROADS *

Tie Tacks ....from.....$ 1.95
Coffee Mugs ....$ 4.95
Belt Buckles ....from.....$ 6.95
T-Shirts (Childs) ....$ 7.95
T-Shirts (Adults) ....$ 8.95
Sweat Shirts (Childs) $12.95
Sweat Shirts (Adults) $15.95
Hats ....$ 7.95
Bumper Stickers ....from....... .79¢
Signs ....from....... .98¢
License Plate Frames ....$ 1.98
Prints ....from.....$ 7.95
Digital Desk Clocks ....$ 9.95
Rubber Stamps ....$ 3.95

* Many other Items

Illustrated Catalog $2.50 (Refund on first order)
Shipping $2.50   MD Residents add 5% tax

*Note: Not every RR name available on every item

**COUNTRY
TRAINS**
WHOLESALE/RETAIL

COUNTRY TRAINS
P.O. Box 1102
Upper Marlboro,
Maryland 20772
(301) 856-3426
Weekdays
11 am - 9 pm

Dealer Inquires Invited

Antiques & Artifacts

Widest selection by mail order of choice RR related things. Museum quality (Smithsonian a regular customer since 1972), authenticity & satisfaction fully guaranteed.

The very best of old RR lanterns, lamps, dining car china & silver, sealers, keys & locks, badges, caps, steam whistles, depot phones, signs, heralds, pocket watches, locomotive builder plates, paperweights, telegraph instruments, daters, Moody's or Poor's manuals, RR cyclopedias, timetables & passes, much more.

Always buying, one item or whole collections. Top cash for real rarities. Consignment arrangements also available. Best bank references and well rated by Dun & Bradstreet. No other RR dealer buys more or sells as much.

Informative illustrated sales publication leads the field & is considered essential reading by many museums, advanced collectors & investors. Send $1. (no envelope) for current issue of the monthly RAILROAD DISPATCH sales catalog.

SCOTT ARDEN

20457 Hwy 126   Noti, OR 97461
503/935-1619 (9am to 6 pm Pacific)
Visitors welcome by
appointment only.

LARGE RAILROAD EMBROIDERED EMBLEMS
12" SIZE FULL-COLOR

These can be framed for your family room,
office, store, or railroad room or worn on
the back of your patch vest or shirt.

*E121   Pennsylvania Railroad
E122   Great Northern
*E123   Union Pacific
E124   New York, New Haven & H.
E125A   The Milwaukee Road

E127   Northern Pacific
E128   Missouri Pacific
E129   Rio Grande.
E130   MKT
E130A   KATY
E131   N.Y.C.
E132   Terminal Railroad of St. Louis
E133   Wabash
E134   Rock Island
E135   Cotton Belt
E136   Illinois Central
E137   Hannibal Connecting
E138   Santa Fe
E139   Reading Lines,
E140   Southern Pacific Lines
E141   Burlington Route,
E142   Pacific Electric,
E143   DTI RR & Ann Arbor RR.
E144   C & O,
E145   C&EI,
E146   C & NW System,
E147   Manufacturers RR of St. Louis,
E199   Twenty (20) all different
             emblems SPECIAL $299.50

MIX OR MATCH ONE $15.95; TWO $31.50;
FOUR $61.95; TEN $149.95
* Add $2.00 per patch for E121 & E123
  ADD $2.00 Per Order for U.P.S.,
    by U.S. Mail add $3.00

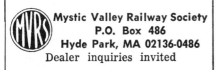

18

Photo by Russell C. Joslin

Location: The Paradise & Pacific R.R. operates at McCormick Railroad Park, 7301 East Indian Bend Road, about 3 miles north of downtown Scottsdale, just off Scottsdale Road. McCormick Railroad Park is owned and operated by the City of Scottsdale.

Ride: Ride through 30 acres of beautiful parkland on a mile of 15" gauge track. The train crosses three trestles and passes a scale ghost town play area during the trip.

Schedule: Train runs Daily, year-round, except Thanksgiving & Christmas Days. Train rides begin at 11:00 A.M.

Fare: Adults & Children over 2, 50¢.

Locomotives: #11, 2-8-2; #12, 2-6-2; #10, 4-6-0. GP-7 switch engine & SW-8 switch engine. All locomotives are 5/12" scale.

Train: Gondola cars modeled after Rio Grande Southern and Denver & Rio Grande Western. Cattle cars of D.&R.G.W., tank car of Colorado & Southern and D.&R.G.W. caboose. All cars are 5/12" scale.
Maricopa Live Steam Club: ¾", 1" and 1½" scales. Also N, HO & O gauge club displays. Static displays include #6, 2-6-0, Baldwin (1907), ex-Magma Arizona R.R.; Pullman observation car "Roald Amundsen", built in 1928; Santa Fe baggage car. Railroad hobby shop, Bill's Trains, located in an 1894 Santa Fe railroad depot. Railroad antique shop, Rails West, located in a 1907 Santa Fe depot.

Roselle Williams, Recreation Coordinator

✔Refreshments
✔Gift Shop
✔Picnic Area
✔Memberships

Paradise & Pacific Railroad
7301 East Indian Bend Road
Scottsdale, AZ 85253
Phone (602) 994-2312

Location: Eureka Springs is in the Ozark Mountain region of northwest Arkansas, a short distance from the Missouri border. The depot is located at the north edge of town on Highway 23 North. Park free at the depot, ride the train, then take the connecting "trolley" through downtown Eureka Springs.

Ride: A 4-mile, 45-minute round trip through a wooded valley next to a winding creek in the heart of the Ozarks. Train crosses four solidly built trestles as it makes its way north.

Schedule: Trains operate Daily, from mid-April through October. Trains depart every hour, on the hour, 10:00 A.M. to 4:00 P.M., seven days a week, rain or shine. Dining car service for breakfast, lunch and dinner is available Daily with departures at 9:00 A.M. (breakfast), 11:00 & 2:00 P.M. (lunch) and 5:00 & 7:00 P.M. (dinner).

Fare: Adults $5.00, Children (5-12) $2.50, under 5 free.

Locomotives: #1, 2-6-0, Baldwin (1906), cabbage-stacked wood-burner, ex-W.T. Carter & Bro.
#201, 2-6-0, Alco (1906), ex-Moscow, Camden & San Augustine. These two locomotives run on alternate days.
Model SW-1 diesel switcher, EMD (1942), ex-C.&E.I. #4742.
#8, 2-truck Shay, Lima (1918).

Train: Steel coaches from Rock Island, wooden Cotton Belt caboose.

Displays: The Eureka Springs depot was built in 1913 of locally cut limestone. It is listed in the National Directory of Historic Places. Turntable from Frisco Lines now in operation.
Robert L. Dortch, President

✔Refreshments
✔Gift Shop
✔Dining Car
✔RV Parking

Eureka Springs & North Arkansas Ry.
P.O. Box 310
Eureka Springs, AR 72632
Phone (501) 253-9623

Photo by W. D. Caileff, Jr.

Location: Trains leave from depot at Reader, off State Route 24 between Camden and Prescott, Ark.

Ride: A 7-mile, 1-hour round trip over the Reader Railroad. Open platform wooden coaches are drawn by veteran logging engines, reminiscent of the railroad's earliest days.

Schedule: Trains operate Saturdays and Sundays, May 2 through August 30. Depart Saturdays at 11:00 A.M. and 2:00 P.M., Sundays at 2:00 P.M. Reservations suggested.

Fare: Adults $6.00, Children (4-11) $3.60, under 4 free with parent. Group rates available.

Locomotives: #7, 2-6-2, Baldwin (1907), ex-Victoria, Fisher & Western.

Train: Open platform wooden coaches, open-air car, caboose. Stove-heated or air ventilated coaches on all trains.

Special Events: Special Night Trains are operated May through September. These trips feature double-headed steam locomotives, dinner and live Bluegrass/Country music. Write for Fall schedule and calendar of special events.

✔Refreshments
✔Gift Shop
✔Picnic Area
✔Park Pavilion

Reader Railroad
P.O. Box 9
Malvern, AR 72104
Phone (501) 337-9591
(501) 624-6881
(501) 685-2692 (Depot)

Location: Bishop is located in eastern California on U.S. Routes 395 and 6. Follow U.S. 6 4½ miles north of Bishop to Silver Canyon Road, then right ½-mile to Museum.

History: In the year 1960, the Southern Pacific R.R. ceased to operate its famed narrow gauge line from Keeler to Laws. Widely known as "The Slim Princess", this little road once wended its way over the mountains to near Carson City, Nevada. At the time of the abandonment, the railroad deeded steam locomotive # 9, the Laws station building, rolling stock and other property to the City of Bishop and Inyo County.

Displays: The Depot, built in 1883, is open to the public as well as the Reception Center and the Station Agent's Residence. Outside is the hand-operated gallows type turntable, used up to the last day of operation. The train, headed by #9, a Baldwin 4-6-0 built in 1909, includes several freight cars and a caboose. Much other narrow gauge rolling stock is on display including a rare two cupola caboose, passenger and freight equipment and a Brill self-propelled car. There are also the Wells Fargo Bldg., Library and Arts Bldg., Assay House and Chalfont Valley General Store. Also Bottle House, Country Store, Doctor's Office, Carriage House and Conway House.

Schedule: Open Daily, March 1 to November 15. Limited schedule, balance of year, weather permitting. Hours are 10:00 A.M. to 4:00 P.M.

Admission: No admission charge. Donations welcome.

✔Refreshments
✔Picnic Area
✔Gift Shop
✔Memberships

Laws Railroad Museum & Historical Site
P.O. Box 363
Bishop, CA 93514
Phone (619) 873-5950

Photo by Daniel C. Robirds

Location: The San Diego & Arizona Ry. is located 50 miles from downtown San Diego. Take Interstate 8 east to Buckman Springs exit and go south 10 miles to State Hwy. 94, then 1 mile west to Campo.

Ride: A 15-mile, 1½-hour round trip from Campo to Miller Creek over the line of the S.D.&A. (ex-S.D.&A.E., ex-S.P.).

Schedule: Saturdays, Sundays and Holidays, year-round. Train leaves Campo at 12:01 P.M. & 2:30 P.M.

Fare: Adults $7.00, Children (5-12) $3.50. Group rates available.

Locomotives: #3, 3-truck Shay, Lima (1923), ex-Hutchinson Lumber.
#1366, H20-44 diesel, F-M (1947), ex-Union Pacific R.R.
#1809, MRS-3 diesel, E.M.D., ex-U.S. Army (SD&A).
#7485, 45-ton diesel, G.E., ex-U.S. Army (SD&A).

Train: Open-window coaches from Santa Fe, Lackawanna and Union Pacific.

Displays: The S.D.&A. is operated by the Pacific Southwest Railway Museum which also has a restored depot at LaMesa.
Large collection at Campo includes:
#11, 2-8-2T, Alco (1929), ex-Coos Bay Lumber Co.;
#46, 2-6-6-2, Baldwin (1937), ex-California Western R.R.;
#2353, 4-6-0, Baldwin (1912), ex-Southern Pacific R.R.;
#104, 2-8-0, Baldwin (1904), ex-Southern Pacific R.R.;
#1, 2-8-0, Baldwin (1897), ex-F.C.Z.; #907, RS-2 diesel, Alco (1949), ex-Kennecott Copper Co. and numerous historic passenger cars, freight and work equipment from area railroads.

James J. Lundquist, Executive Director

✔Refreshments
✔Gift Shop
✔Picnic Area

TRAIN

San Diego & Arizona Railway
P.O. Box 509
Campo, CA 92006
Phone (619) 478-9937
(619) 69-PSRMA (taped info)

Location: Felton is 80 miles south of San Francisco, 30 miles west of San Jose. Depot is located on Graham Hill Road in Felton.

Ride: A 6-mile, 1¼-hour trip behind a narrow-gauge locomotive up steep grades and around sharp curves. The train climbs an 8% grade through the redwoods and winds around horseshoe loops to the summit of Bear Mountain. At Spring Canyon, the track climbs up the mountainside on a spectacular double switchback track.

Schedule: Roaring Camp is open year-round, except Christmas Day. Trains run Daily, lv Noon. Additional trains operate on weekends and holidays. Daily, June 13 to September 7, trains lv. 11:00 A.M., 12:15, 1:30, 2:45, 4:00 P.M. On Saturday evenings, June through October, Moonlight Steam Train Parties operate. Reservations required.

Fare: Adults $10.00, Children (3-15) $7.00, under 3 free.

Locomotives: #1, 2-truck Shay, Lima (1912), ex-Coal Processing Corp. #2593.
     #2, 2-truck Heisler, (1899), ex-West Side Lumber Co. #3.
     #4, 0-6-2T, Baldwin (1897), ex-Oahu Sugar Co., Ltd #1.
     #5, 2-truck Climax, (1928), ex-Elk River Coal & Lumber #3.
     #7, 3-truck Shay, Lima (1910), ex-West Side & Cherry Valley Ry. #4.
     #40, diesel switcher, Plymouth (1958), ex-Kaiser Steel Co. #2.

Train: Open excursion type cars, side door caboose, observation car.

Displays: At Roaring Camp is an 1880 general store, covered bridge, Red Caboose Saloon, Chuckwagon barbeque, operating steam sawmill and next door is Henry Cowell Redwoods State Park. In 1986, over 1000 tour groups from more than 30 countries visited Roaring Camp to ride the historic steam train through the redwood forests.

✔Refreshments		R.C. & B.T.N.G.R.R.
✔Gift Shop		P.O. Box 338
✔Picnic Area		Felton, CA 95018
✔Camp Grounds adjacent		Phone (408) 335-4400

CALIFORNIA, FELTON
Santa Cruz, Big Trees & Pacific Ry.

Location: Depot is located at Roaring Camp, on Graham Hill Road, in Felton.

Ride: A 14-mile, 2½-hour round trip along the spectacular San Lorenzo River Canyon to the beach at Santa Cruz. Train travels across trestles and bridges, through a tunnel, past the fabled Big Trees stand of California Redwoods, and down quiet streets lined with Victorian homes in Santa Cruz. Plans are currently underway to operate a steam locomotive on the line.

Schedule: Train operates on Saturdays, Sundays & Holidays during Spring and Fall, Daily during the Summer. Departs Roaring Camp at 11:30 A.M. & 2:30 P.M. Additional trains may operate, depending on the season.

Fare: Adults $15.00, Children (3-15) $7.50.
Passengers may originate at either Roaring Camp or Santa Cruz.

Locomotives: #2640, 2641, CF-7 diesels, ex-Santa Fe.
Steam locomotive, to be announced.

Train: Five 1920's era passenger coaches, two open-air cars and restored 1895 caboose from Lake Superior & Ishpeming R.R.

Note: This line, once considered one of the most scenic railroads in the West, was originally built in 1875 as the Santa Cruz & Felton R.R. Later it became the South Pacific Coast R.R. and then a branch of the Southern Pacific. Purchased in 1985 by F. Norman Clark, late President of Roaring Camp, Inc., it is operated as an historic railroad.

✔Refreshments
✔Gift Shop
✔Picnic Area
✔Camp Grounds adjacent

Santa Cruz, Big Trees & Pacific R.R.
P.O. Box G-1
Felton, CA 95018
Phone (408) 335-4400

CALIFORNIA, FISH CAMP   Steam, scheduled
Yosemite Mountain - Sugar Pine R.R.   36" gauge

Photo by Joseph T. Bispo

Location: On Highway 41, four miles south of Yosemite National Park.

Ride: A 4-mile, 45-minute round trip over the restored line of the Madera Sugar Pine Co. railroad. Track runs through the Sierra Nevada mountains at a 5000 ft. elevation, winds down a 4% grade deep into Lewis Creek Canyon passing Horseshoe Curve, over Cold Spring Crossing and stopping at Slab Creek Loop. Passengers may stop over here and return by a later train.

Schedule: STEAM: Week-ends, May 23-25 and June 6 thru September 7. Departures at 10:30 A.M., Noon, 1:30 & 3:30 P.M. Special week-day trips: August 3-28 at 11:00 A.M. & Noon. Fall Excursions: Week-ends, September 12 thru October 12 at 11:00 A.M. & Noon.
RAILCARS: Daily, April 12 thru October 31 (except when steam train operates).

Fare: Steam train: Adults $6.75, Children $3.75.
Railcars: Adults $4.75, Children $2.75.

Locomotives: #10, 3-truck Shay, Lima (1928), ex-West Side Lumber Co. This is the largest narrow-gauge Shay engine ever built.
#15, 3-truck Shay, Lima (1913), ex-West Side Lumber Co.
#5, 10-ton gas-mechanical with diesel engine, Vulcan.
Two Model A powered railcars.

Train: Logging cars with quarter-sawn logs forming benches.

Note: Moonlite Special: Western style BBQ, live entertainment, Saturday nights in summer. Reservations advised.

Displays: Logging display with steam donkey engine. Also museum and craft shops. The railroad operates on a U.S. Forest Service Special Use Permit. Located next door is the Narrow-Gauge Inn offering food and lodging with turn of the century atmosphere.

Max Stauffer, President

✔Refreshments
✔Gift Shop
✔Picnic Area
✔Arts & Crafts

Yosemite Mountain - Sugar Pine R.R.
Fish Camp, CA 93623
Phone (209) 683-7273

CALIFORNIA, FORT BRAGG
California Western R.R.

Diesel, Steam, scheduled
Standard gauge

Location: The California Western R.R. extends from Fort Bragg on the Pacific coast 40 miles inland to Willits on Highway 101.

Ride: "Super Skunk" passenger trains operate from Fort Bragg and from Willits. Both short 3-4 hour and longer 7½-8½ hour trips are available. Shorter trips operate to Northspur, halfway along the line. The railroad runs through highly scenic terrain in redwood forests remote from roads or towns.

Schedule: "Super Skunk" operates Daily, June 20 thru September 12. Lv. Fort Bragg 9:20 A.M. & 1:35 P.M. Lv. Willits 8:50 A.M. & 1:45 P.M. Steam locomotive will operate on special dates, call Depot for info. Half-day Northspur trips also operate Saturdays, April - June and September - October. The line's famous "Skunk" railcars operate Daily, September 13 thru June 17, 1988 (except Thanksgiving, Christmas & New Years Day).

Fare: "Super Skunk" to Northspur: Adults $16.00, Children (5-11) $8.00. "Super Skunk" entire line: Adults $20.00, Children (5-11) $10.00. Reservations recommended.

Locomotives: #45, 2-8-2, Baldwin (1924), ex-Medford Corp.
#55 and #56, RS-12 diesels, Baldwin (1955), ex-McCloud River R.R.

Train: Stilwell coaches from Erie Railroad, Southern Pacific coaches, open observation cars.

Note: Write for comprehensive timetables enclosing a large SASE.

✔Refreshments
✔Gift Shop
✔Picnic Area

California Western R.R.
P.O. Box 907
Fort Bragg, CA 95437
Phone (707) 964-6371

CALIFORNIA, FREMONT
Pacific Locomotive Assn., Inc.

Steam, Diesel, irregular
Standard gauge

Photo by D.E. Burla

Location: The large collection of locomotives and rolling stock of the Pacific Locomotive Assn. is being moved to a new location at Niles Canyon, in the Fremont-Sunol region. The site is about 40 minutes from San Francisco and 20 minutes from San Jose. Historic Niles Canyon was one of the last links in the transcontinental railroad (Central Pacific/Southern Pacific).

Schedule: Operation on an initial two miles of trackage is expected to begin in June 1987. Write the Pacific Locomotive Assn. at the address below for schedule information.

Locomotives: Serviceable
> #2, 2-6-2T, Schenectady (1924), ex-Quincy R.R.
> #3, 0-4-0T, Porter (1913), ex-Steptoe Valley Mining Co.
> #4, 2-6-6-2T, Baldwin (1924), ex-Clover Valley Lumber Co.
> #5, 3-truck Heisler (1913), ex-Pickering Lumber Co.
> #12, 3-truck Shay, Lima (1903), ex-Pickering Lumber Co.
> #462, 44-ton diesel-electric, G.E. (1943), ex-A.T.&S.F.
> M-200, Motor Car, ex-California Western R.R.
> #713, GP-7 diesel, E.M.D. (1950), ex-Western Pacific.

Under restoration:
> #7, 3-truck Shay, Lima (1925), ex-Pickering Lumber Co.
> #1, 3-truck Heisler (1913), ex-Pickering Lumber Co.
> #30, 2-6-2, Baldwin (1922), ex-Sierra R.R.
> #233, 2-6-2T, Central Pacific Shops (1882), ex-C.P.R.R.
> #918, F7A diesel-electric, E.M.D. (1950), ex-Western Pacific.

Train: Harriman R.P.O., coaches, freight cars, caboose.

Pacific Locomotive Association
P.O. Box 2247, Niles Station
Fremont, CA 94536
Phone (415) 653-0354

Location: The Museum is located at 250th & Woodward Ave. at Lomita just south of Los Angeles.

Displays: The museum, built in 1966, is an exact replica of the Boston & Maine station at Wakefield, Mass. Donated to the City of Lomita by Mrs. Irene Lewis, no expense was spared to create a suitable treasury for the railroad artifacts on display. Shown here are many live steam models as well as a huge and important collection of railroadiana. The station agent's office is complete in every respect. Outside, a Southern Pacific "Mogul" steam locomotive and a Union Pacific caboose wait at the station's platforms.

Locomotives: #1765, 2-6-0, Baldwin (1902), ex-Southern Pacific with a large whaleback tender.

Schedule: Wednesday through Sunday, year-round. Open 10:00 A.M. to 5:00 P.M. Closed Monday and Tuesday. Closed Christmas Day.

Admission: Adults, Children 50¢.

Rolling Stock: Union Pacific caboose No. 25730, Class CA-1, built in 1910. A 1913 wooden boxcar and a 1923 oil tank car are also on display at our Annex park. A charming recreation park for general public enjoyment with a decor of benches, water fountain, lights and brickwork of the Victorian era.

Arthur W. Zimmerla, Curator

✔Gift Shop   Lomita Railroad Museum
✔Picnic Area   250th & Woodward Ave.
                              Lomita, CA 90717
                              Phone (213) 326-6255

Location: Travel Town is located in Griffith Park, the city's largest park, at the intersection of the Golden State Freeway (I-5) and the Ventura Freeway (I-134). The Museum is located at the north end of the Park on Forest Lawn Drive.

Displays: The railroad exhibits consist of a number of outdoor tracks on which are placed about 14 steam locomotives, an electric engine, passenger cars and trolleys.

Locomotives: Engines on display include #1, 4-4-0, Norris (1867), ex-Stockton Terminal & Eastern; #664, 2-8-0, Baldwin (1899), ex-Santa Fe; #3025, 4-4-2, Alco (1904), ex-Southern Pacific; #1544, steeple-cab electric (1902), ex-Pacific Electric.

Ride: Travel Town R.R. offers a one-mile ride, twice around the Museum in a one-third scale train. Replica Southern Pacific locomotive and 6 open passenger cars operate every day.

Schedule: Travel Town is open Daily, 9:00 A.M. to 5:00 P.M. Train operates Daily (except Christmas Day).

Fare: Park admission free. Train ride: Adults $1.50, Children $1.25. Group rates available.

Note: At the Los Feliz entrance to Griffith Park is the Griffith Park & Southern R.R., one-third scale replica steam and diesel trains which operate every day. Both trains are owned and operated by Railroad Supply Corp.

✔Refreshments
✔Gift Shop
✔Picnic Area
Amtrak ➤➤➤ Los Angeles

Railroad Supply Corp.
115 S. Victory Blvd.
Burbank, CA 91502
Phone (213) 849-1351

Location: At 2201 South "A" Street in Perris, about 18 miles southeast of Riverside on Interstate I-215. The Museum is one mile south of Perris, which has Greyhound bus service from Los Angeles and San Diego.

Ride: Interurbans and trains operate over a 2-mile former railroad right-of-way, and streetcars operate on a half-mile route around the Museum grounds.

Schedule: Saturdays, Sundays and public school holidays (except Thanksgiving and Christmas), year-round, 11:00 A.M. to 5:00 P.M. or dusk. Daily, Palm Sunday-Easter Sunday and December 26-January 1. Special events, Rail Festival in April, Fall Festival in October, Spring and Fall Swap Meets. Write for dates.

Fare: Unlimited rides and guided tour: Adults $3.50, Children (6-11) $2.00, under 6 free. Family rate $12.50.

Locomotives: #2, 2-6-2, Baldwin (1922), ex-Ventura County R.R.
   #653, General Electric (1928), ex-Sacramento Northern.
   #1624, P.E. Shops (1925), ex-Pacific Electric.
   #8580, General Electric (1944), ex-U.S. Air Force.

Trolleys: #498, ex-Pacific Electric. #3165, ex-Los Angeles Transit Lines. #665, #1160, #1201, #3100, ex-Los Angeles Ry. #19, ex-Kyoto (Japan) Street Ry.

Train: Santa Fe and Union Pacific coaches, Santa Fe RPO car, Union Pacific caboose.

Displays: Over 150 pieces of equipment are displayed here, including streetcars, interurbans, work cars, electric, steam and diesel locomotives, passenger cars and freight cars.

✔Refreshments   Orange Empire Railway Museum
✔Gift Shop   P.O. Box 548
✔Picnic Area   Perris, CA 92370
✔Memberships   Phone (714) 657-2605
                                              (Recorded information)

CALIFORNIA, PORTOLA
Portola Railroad Museum

Photo by John J. Ryczkowski

Location: Portola is located 50 miles northwest of Reno, Nevada in the Feather River country of the Sierra Nevada Mountains. On the main-line of the former Western Pacific R.R., the site is near the Feather River Canyon. The Museum is located in the former Western Pacific diesel service facility west of the Portola depot. From State Route 70, go one mile on County Road A-15 (Gulling) south across river through town, follow signs.

Ride: A one-mile ride around a balloon turning track through pine forest.

Schedule: Museum is open Daily from Memorial Day to last week-end of September from 10:00 A.M. to 5:00 P.M. Open week-ends, rest of year. Train operates on the last week-end of the month, May through September, every half-hour from 10:00 A.M. to 4:00 P.M.

Fare: Adults $2.00 each, Family ticket $5.00, good all day.
Admission to museum free, donations welcome.

Locomotives: #8, 2-6-2, Baldwin (1907), ex-Clover Valley Lumber Co.
#2, #3, RS-3 diesels, Alco (1950), ex-Kennecott Copper.
#608, NW-2 diesel, EMC (1940); #708, GP-7 diesel, EMD (1952), ex-W.P.R.R. #778, Electric, GE (1955), ex-Kennecott Minerals.
#921-D, F-7A, EMD (1950); #2001, GP-20, EMD (1959), ex-W.P.R.R.
#3051, U30B diesel, GE (1967), ex-W.P.R.R.
#6946, DDA-40X, EMD, ex-U.P.R.R. Centennial diesel.
#1506, 1507, 1508, F-7A, EMD, ex-Alaska R.R.
#1510, 1512, FP-7, EMD, #1517, F-7B, ex-Alaska R.R.

Train: Steam or diesel locomotive with cabooses and vista-flat cars.

Displays: Over 50 freight cars, representing nearly every Western Pacific car type, several passenger cars and other rolling stock. Railroad artifacts on display in diesel shop building.
Norman W. Holmes, President

✔Refreshments
✔Gift Shop
✔Memberships

Feather River Rail Society
P.O. Box 8
Portola, CA 96122
Phone (916) 832-4131

CALIFORNIA, RIO VISTA JCT.
Bay Area Electric Railroad Assn.
Western Railway Museum

Electric, scheduled
Steam, irregular
Standard gauge

Photo by Vernon J. Sappers

Location: On Route 12 midway between Fairfield and Rio Vista in Solano County. Site is about 55 miles northeast of San Francisco.

Ride: A 2-mile, 20-minute ride past the picnic area and some 100 electric and steam railroad exhibits on the Museum's grounds.

Schedule: Electric cars operate Saturdays, Sundays & Holiday Mondays, year-round from 11:00 A.M. to 5:00 P.M. Steam or diesel trains will operate several week-ends during the year.

Admission: Adults $3.00; Youths (12-17) & Seniors (over 65) $2.00; Children (3-11) $1.00; Tots Free.

Locomotives: #94, 4-6-0, Alco (1909), ex-Western Pacific R.R.; #334, 2-8-2, Alco (1929), ex-Western Pacific R.R.; #3, 2-6-2T, Alco (1927), ex-Robert Dollar Lumber Co.; #2978, 2-truck Shay, Lima (1918), ex-Robert Dollar Co.; ex-Western Pacific F-unit #917. #1001, steeple cab electric (1910), ex-Key System; #654, freight motor, G.E. (1931), ex-Sacramento Northern; #502, 44-ton diesel, G.E. (1944), ex-Visalia Electric; #711, GP-7 diesel, ex-Sacramento Northern.

Electric Cars: #578, built 1895 for Market St. Ry. Co.; #178, San Francisco Municipal Ry.; #62, Sacramento Northern Birney; #202, Portland Traction suburban car; #987, Key System streetcar; #1003, San Francisco "Magic Carpet Car"; "Open Boat" tram from Blackpool, England; #271, Key System, former Lehigh Valley Transit streetcar; #111, Cincinnati & Lake Erie interurban; 3 P.C.C. cars; #63, Petaluma & Santa Rosa interurban; #52, Peninsular Ry. interurban; #1005, Sacramento Northern interurban; Melbourne streetcar #648; Key System Bay Bridge trains.

Displays: Over 80 different historic cars including 1886 New York City "El" cars, Napa Valley interurban #63, Pullman heavyweight lounge car #653 and Niles built observation "Champoeg".

Vernon J. Sappers, Museum Curator

✔Refreshments
✔Book Store
✔Picnic Area
✔Memberships

Bay Area Electric R.R. Assn.
P.O. Box 3694
San Francisco, CA 94119
Phone (707) 374-2978 (Week-ends)

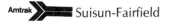 Suisun-Fairfield

33

Displays: This is the finest interpretive railroad museum in North America, featuring over 30 meticulously restored locomotives and cars from the beginning of railroading in the West to the present day. The $20 million state railroad museum complex is located on an 11 acre site in Old Sacramento. The Museum includes the reconstructed 1870's Central Pacific R.R. freight and passenger stations, the Big Four Building, the Library-Archive and the Museum of Railroad History.

Schedule: Open Daily, 10:00 A.M. to 5:00 P.M.

Admission: Adults $3.00, Children (6-17) $1.00, under 6 free.

Locomotives: Perfectly restored engines here range from the tiny "C.P. Huntington", a 4-2-4T built by Cooke in 1863, Southern Pacific's Engine No. 1; Central Pacific locomotive No. 1, the "Gov. Stanford" is a Norris 4-4-0 built in 1862. There are 3 Virginia & Truckee engines, "Genoa", "Empire" and "J.W. Bowker". Larger power includes Santa Fe #1010, 2-6-2, Baldwin (1901) which powered a portion of Death Valley Scotty's famous high-speed run. Southern Pacific's giant cab-forward #4294, 4-8-8-2, Baldwin (1944) dwarfs some of the smaller engines. Diesel power includes Western Pacific F-7 diesel #913, Southern Pacific E-9A passenger diesel #6051 and Sacramento Northern SW-1 #402.

Rolling Stock: There are numerous restored passenger, mail and freight cars. The sleeping car "St. Hyacinthe" gives the illusion of speeding through the night, with simulated sound, light and motion. A Great Northern Railway Post Office car is completely equipped. Beebe & Clegg's famous private car, the "Gold Coast" is on display along with many others. A complete narrow-gauge freight train is exhibited on a bridge high above the museum floor. The interpretive displays place the visitor into the individual scene through very effective visual and audio methods.

Ronald L. Hanshew, Director

✔Station Restaurant
✔Museum Bookstore
✔Guided Tours

California State Railroad Museum
111 "I" Street
Sacramento, CA 95814
Phone (916) 448-4466

 Sacramento

Location: Steam trains operate from the reconstructed Central Pacific R.R. Freight Depot at Front and K Streets in Old Sacramento.

Ride: A 6-mile, 50-minute round trip along the historic Sacramento River. Future expansion is planned to the towns of Freeport and Hood, 16 miles down the river.

Schedule: Saturdays, Sundays & Holidays, May through Labor Day (except July 4-5). Trains leave on the hour between 10:00 A.M. and 5:00 P.M.

Fare: Adults $3.00, Children (6-17) $2.00, under 6 free. Caboose charters, special trains and group rates available, write for information.

Locomotives: #4466, 0-6-0, Lima (1920), ex-Union Pacific R.R. #1269, 0-6-0, Sacramento (1921), ex-Southern Pacific R.R.

Train: Open and closed excursion type cars.

Displays: The steam train operation is a part of the ongoing activities of the California State Railroad Museum.

Ronald L. Hanshew, Director

California State Railroad Museum
Sacramento Southern R.R.
111 "I" Street
Sacramento, CA 95814
Phone (916) 448-4466

Photo by Kermit Parker

Location: Sonoma is in the wine country, less than an hour north of San Francisco. Train Town is located on Broadway, 1 mile south of Sonoma's Town Square.

Ride: Train Town is a 10-acre railroad park filled with thousands of trees, animals, lakes, bridges, tunnels and historic replica structures. 15" gauge live-steam locomotives and diesel replicas pull long passenger trains through the park.

Schedule: Saturdays and Sundays year-round from 11:00 A.M. to 5:00 P.M. Also open Daily, mid-June through Labor Day.

Fare: Adults $2.20, Seniors & Children under 16, $1.60.

Locomotives: #5212, 4-6-4, Alco (1937). This exact scale model of a New York Central J-1a Hudson type was built by the American Locomotive Works for Paul W. Kiefer, Superintendent of Motive Power of the New York Central System, rebuilt by Bob Callendar in 1953.
#1, 2-6-0, built by Winton Engineering in 1960 and rebuilt by Rick Mugele in 1983.
#401, gas-electric motor car, built by Kermit R. Parker in 1975.

Train: There are a total of 16 passenger and freight cars, all accurate scale reproductions built by Stanley L. Frank.

Displays: Railroad shops and a complete miniature town, all built to the same ¼" scale as the railroad. Full size rail equipment includes Santa Fe caboose 999648, Union Pacific caboose 25155 and Southern Pacific's first steel caboose #11.

✔Refreshments   Train Town
✔Gift Shop   P.O. Box 656
                                                        Sonoma, CA 95476
                                                    Phone (707) 938-3912

COLORADO, CRIPPLE CREEK   Steam, scheduled
Cripple Creek Narrow Gauge R.R.   24" gauge

Location: Steam-powered two-foot gauge trains leave from the former Midland Terminal R.R.'s Bull Hill depot in the historic mining town of Cripple Creek.

Ride: A 4-mile, 45-minute round trip over a portion of the old Midland Terminal R.R. The little train runs south out of Cripple Creek, past the old MT wye, over a reconstructed trestle, past many historic mines to the deserted mining town of Anaconda.

Schedule: Daily, May 23 to October 9, 1987. Train leaves every 45 minutes from 10:00 A.M. to 5:30 P.M.

Fare: Adults $4.75, Children $2.75, under 3 free.

Locomotives: #1, 0-4-4-0, Orenstein & Koppel (1902); #2, 0-4-0, Henschel (1936); #3, 0-4-0T, Porter (1927); #13, 0-4-4-0T, Bagnall (1946).

Train: Open excursion type cars.

Displays: A museum is located in the former Midland Terminal depot.

✔Gift Shop   Cripple Creek Narrow Gauge R.R.
✔Refreshments   Box 459
                              Cripple Creek, CO 80813
                                                       Phone (303) 689-2640

COLORADO, DENVER
Forney Historic Transportation Museum

Railway Museum
Standard gauge

Photo by Michael A. Eagleson

Location: The Forney Museum is located at Valley Highway (I-25) and Speer Blvd. in Denver. From I-25 use Exit 212C southbound or Exit 211 northbound.

Displays: The railroad exhibit at the Forney Museum features three steam locomotives. Union Pacific "Big Boy" #4005, built by Alco in 1941, is on display outside the main building. Nearby is #444, a 4-6-0 from the Chicago & North Western Ry. and inside is an 0-4-0T locomotive from Germany. There are four executive and business cars, two of which were built in the 1890's, also a dining car. The collection also includes a rotary snow plow and two cabooses. The Museum has a fine collection of horse-drawn vehicles and a large display of antique automobiles.

Schedule: Open Daily (except Thanksgiving and Christmas Day). May through October, 9:00 A.M. to 5:00 P.M., Sundays 11:00 A.M. to 5:00 P.M. November through April, 9:30 A.M. to 5:00 P.M., Sundays 11:00 A.M. to 5:00 P.M.

Admission: Adults $3.00, Children (12-18) $1.50 & (5-11) 50¢.
Group rates available.

Jack Forney, President
Jean Stokes, Manager

✔Refreshments
✔Gift Shop
✔Picnic Area

Forney Historic Transportation Museum
1416 Platte St.
Denver, CO 80202
Phone (303) 433-3643

Amtrak ➤ Denver

COLORADO, DENVER
Union Pacific R.R.

Steam, irregular
Standard gauge

Photo by Michael A. Eagleson

Ride: A spectacular all-day rail excursion powered by Union Pacific's #8444. The train will operate from Denver to Laramie, Wyoming and return. Several photo stops will be made during the course of the trip.

Schedule: Trip will operate on Saturday, October 3, 1987. Train will leave Denver Union Station at 7:30 A.M., return 8:00 P.M.

Fare: Adults $185.00, Children $175.00. Fare includes box lunch. Tickets should be ordered as early as possible, as trip is expected to sell out in a short time.

Locomotives: #8444, 4-8-4, Alco (1942), Union Pacific R.R.

Train: Union Pacific open-door baggage car, streamlined coaches, dome car and lounge car.

Intermountain Chapter, N.R.H.S.
General Passenger Agent
P.O. Box 5181, Terminal Annex
Denver, CO 80217

Denver

39

COLORADO, DURANGO
Durango & Silverton Narrow-Gauge R.R.

Steam, scheduled
36" gauge

Photo by John E. Helbok

Location: Durango is located in the southwestern part of Colorado, on U.S. 160.

Ride: Steam-powered narow-gauge trains travel through the remote wilderness of San Juan National Forest, following the winding Animas River through breathtaking mountain scenery. Much of the route is accessible only by rail or horseback. The 90-mile round trip from Durango to Silverton and back takes 9 hours, including a 2¼-hour stop at Silverton. Advance reservations are recommended.

Schedule: Train operates from May 9 through October 25, 1987. Leave Durango 8:30 & 9:30 A.M. Additional trains operate at 7:30 & 10:15 A.M. June through August. Consult timetable for exact schedule on day of your visit.

Fare: Adults $28.10, Children (5-11) $14.10, Parlor Car $48.30.

Locomotives: #473, 476, 478, 2-8-2's, Alco (1923), Class K-28.
#480, 481, 2-8-2, Baldwin (1925), Class K-36.
#493, 497, 498, 499, 2-8-2, Burnham Shops (1930), Class K-37.
All locomotives ex-Denver & Rio Grande Western R.R.

Train: Coaches, open-side observation cars, coach for disabled, parlor car.

Note: Due to long lines at the station, it is recommended that tickets be purchased by mail or reserved in advance. Write for comprehensive brochure and complete timetables.

✔Refreshments on train
✔Gift Shop
✔Restaurants at Silverton

Durango & Silverton Narrow-Gauge R.R.
479 Main Avenue
Durango, CO 81301
Phone (303) 247-2733

COLORADO, FALCON
Cadillac & Lake City Ry.

Diesel, scheduled
Standard gauge

Location: Trains depart from Falcon, 15 miles east of Colorado Springs on U.S. 24. The Cadillac & Lake City operates a 67-mile line from Limon to Colorado Springs over former Rock Island trackage, once traversed by the famed "Rocky Mountain Rocket".

Ride: Trips vary from an 18-mile, 1¼-hour run to Peyton and back, to an all-day, 120-mile roundtrip to Limon. The train travels over the high plains in full sight of Pikes Peak and the Rocky Mountains.

Schedule: To Peyton, Saturdays & Sundays, June 20-21 & 27-28, then Wednesdays through Sundays during July and August. Trains leave Falcon at 1:00 & 2:30 P.M.
"Twilight Limited" runs to Calhan Fridays & Saturdays during July and August at 7:00 P.M. Dessert served aboard train.

Fare: To Peyton: Adults $5.95, Seniors $4.95, Children $2.95.
Other fares based on length of trip.

Locomotives: #48 & #50, CF-7 diesels, ex-Santa Fe.

Train: Rio Grande and Milwaukee Road coaches, New York Central parlor car.

Special Events: Trips to Limon May 25 (Memorial Day) and September 7 (Labor Day), both Mixed Train Daily. Railfans' Week-end September 12 & 13. El Paso County Fair Trains to Calhan July 30 to August 2. Numerous other special events, call or write for information.

Myra J. Noble, General Passenger Agent

✔Refreshments
✔Gift Shop
✔Memberships in Train Crew

Mailing Address:
Cadillac & Lake City Ry.
121 E. Pikes Peak Ave. Suite 224A
Colorado Springs, CO 80903
Phone (303) 634-1091

41

COLORADO, FORT COLLINS
Fort Collins Municipal Railway

Electric, scheduled
Standard gauge

Location: Fort Collins is located on I-25 in the northern part of the State. The streetcar operates on West Mountain Ave. Take Exit 269-B of I-25, proceed west on State Rte. 14 to Mountain Ave., then west on that street.

Ride: A 1½-mile round trip on a restored portion of the historic Fort Collins trolley system. The tracks are in a grass median down the center of Mountain Ave., then down the center of Roosevelt Ave. to the City Park. Passengers board at the City Park terminus.

Schedule: Saturdays, Sundays & Holidays, April through October, weather permitting. Car operates from Noon to 6:00 P.M. Group charters and special rates available.

Fare: Adults $1.00, Children (under 12) 25¢.

Trolleys: #21, single-truck Birney Safety Car, American Car (1919). This car was purchased new by the City of Fort Collins and was in daily service until 1951.

Note: The Fort Collins Municipal Railway Society is a non-profit group of volunteers. The streetcar and railway are the property of the City of Fort Collins. The painstakingly restored car is on the National Register of Historic Places.

✔Picnic Area
✔Memberships

Fort Collins Municipal Railway
P.O. Box 635
Fort Collins, CO 80522
Phone (303) 493-7199
(303) 224-5372 (week-ends)

COLORADO, GEORGETOWN
Georgetown Loop R.R.

Photo by John E. Helbok

Location: Trains leave from Georgetown or Silver Plume in the historic mining district west of Denver on Interstate 70. Use Exit 226 for Silver Plume, Exit 228 for Georgetown.

Ride: A 6½-mile, 1-hr. 10 min. trip over the right-of-way of the old Colorado & Southern narrow-gauge line. The train travels over the newly reconstructed Devil's Gate Viaduct, a spectacular 96 ft. high curved trestle. The line runs through highly scenic, mountainous terrain. The Georgetown Loop Railroad is a project of the Colorado State Historical Society.

Schedule: Daily operation, May 23 through September 7, 1987.
Lv. Silver Plume: (round trip) 10:00, 11:20, 12:40, 2:00, 3:20, 4:40 P.M.
Lv. Georgetown: (round trip) 10:40, 12:00, 1:20, 2:40, 4:00 P.M.

Fare: Adults $7.50, Children (5-15) $3.75, under 5 free.
Diesel-powered charter trips available year-round.

Locomotives: #40, 2-8-0, Baldwin (1920), #44, 2-8-0, Baldwin (1921), both ex-International Railways of Central America.
#8, 3-truck Shay, Lima (1922), #12, 3-truck Shay, Lima (1926).
#14, 3-truck Shay, Lima (1916), all ex-West Side Lumber Co.
#15, 47-ton diesel, G.E. (1943), ex-Oahu Railway & Land Co.

Train: Open excursion type cars and caboose.

Displays: The Colorado State Historical Society's mine tour and exhibit will be open and can be reached by train. Allow an additional 1 hr. 20 min. for the tour at a cost of Adults $2.50, Children $1.25.

Lindsey G. Ashby, General Manager

✔Gift Shop

Georgetown Loop Railroad
P.O. Box 217
Georgetown, CO 80444
Phone (303) 279-6101 (Recorded message)
(303) 569-2403 (Summer)

Denver

Photo by Thomas R. Schultz

Location: The Museum is located 12 miles west of Denver at the foot of the first mountain. Take Exit 265 off I-70 to 17155 W. 44 Ave. between Wheat Ridge and Golden.

Displays: The 29-year-old museum, oldest and largest in the Rocky Mountain area, houses an extensive collection of Colorado railroad memorabilia, as well as the layout of the Denver HO Model Railroad Club. On the outdoor trackage are over 50 pieces of rolling stock, primarily narrow-gauge, including the oldest locomotives and cars in the state.

Schedule: Open year-round, seven days a week from 9:00 A.M. to 5:00 P.M. During June, July & August, the Museum is open until 6:00 P.M.

Admission: Adults $2.50, Seniors $2.00, Children (under 16) $1.00. Family rate (parents & children under 16) $5.50.

Locomotives: #346, 2-8-0, Baldwin (1881), ex-D.&R.G.W, will operate week-ends of May 23-25, July 11-12, August 22-23, October 3-4 and Santa Claus trips December 5-6.

Train: On the above dates 2 and possibly 3 Rio Grande Southern "Galloping Geese" will be operated.

Rolling Stock: Passenger cars, freight cars, locomotives and trolley cars are on display. Burlington Route 4-8-4 #5629 is joined by both standard and narrow-gauge Rio Grande engines and cars.

✔Refreshments
✔Gift Shop
✔Picnic Area

Colorado Railroad Museum
P.O. Box 10
Golden, CO 80402
Phone (303) 279-4591

 Denver

44

COLORADO, GOLDEN
High Country R.R.

Steam, scheduled
24" gauge

Photo by James L. Ehernberger

Location: Trains operate from Heritage Square, located about 15 minutes west of Denver. From I-70, exit at Morrison & Red Rocks interchange and go ½-mile north on U.S. 40.

Ride: A 1½-mile, 15-minute ride over a loop of track winding around the scenic foothills of the Rockies. Route goes through cuts, over high fills and trestles, round a lake and through a snowshed. Excellent views of Denver and Golden can be seen from the train.

Schedule: Daily, Memorial through Labor Day, 11:00 A.M. to sunset. Weekends, April, May, September and October, weather permitting.

Fare: Adults $2.50, Children $1.50, under 5 free.

Locomotives: #01, 4-wheel "Tom Thumb" type
    #1, 0-4-0T, Orenstein & Koppel (1901)
    #4, Plymouth diesel (1933)
    #6, 2-truck Shay, Lima (1920)
    #8, 0-8-0T, Hartmann (1918)
    #9, 0-4-0T, Henschel (1939)

Train: Open excursion cars, coach and private car.

Displays: Heritage Square contains numerous amusement rides and has a variety of shops, stores and eating spots, housed in period type buildings.

At Heritage Square
✔Refreshments
✔Gift Shop
✔Restaurant

Mailing Address:
High Country Railroad
1540 Routt Street
Lakewood, CO 80215

 Denver

COLORADO, MANITOU SPRINGS
Manitou & Pike's Peak Railway

Diesel, scheduled
Standard gauge (cog)

Location: At Colorado Springs, take exit from I-25 west on U.S. 24 to Manitou Springs. Exit U.S. 24 at signs for Cog R.R. Take Manitou Ave. to Ruxton Ave. Turn left one mile.

Ride: This world famous cog railway has been taking passengers to the summit of Pike's Peak since 1891. The 18-mile round trip takes 3 hrs. 10 min. (40 minutes sightseeing at top of Pike's Peak). The trip begins in heavily forested Engleman Canyon and ends at the 14,110 ft. summit. This is the highest railroad in the United States and the highest cog railway in the world.

Schedule: Daily, May through October. Departs 9:20 A.M. & 1:20 P.M. Mid-June through August, trains leave every 80 minutes, 8:00 A.M. to 5:20 P.M.

Fare: Adults $15.00, Children (5-11) $7.00, under 5 free.
Reservations are advised at all times.

Train: All passenger trains are self-contained Diesel railcars running on cog track with grades between 8 & 25%.
Nos. 14, 15, 16, 17 are Swiss built Diesel-electrics (1963).
Nos. 18, 19, and 24 are Swiss built Diesel-hydraulic (1976-1984).

Locomotives: M.&P.P. Ry. #4, Baldwin (1897) has been restored for use. M.&P.P. Ry. #5, Baldwin (1901) is on display at depot.

Notes: Summit House at top of Pike's Peak has coffee shop and souvenirs. Across the street from the Cog Ry. depot is the Mt. Manitou Incline. This is a cable-operated line with maximum grades of 68%.

✔Refreshments
✔Gift Shop

Manitou & Pike's Peak Railway
P.O. Box 1329
Colorado Springs, CO 80901
Phone (303) 685-5401

CONNECTICUT, EAST HAVEN
Shore Line Trolley Museum

Electric, scheduled
Standard gauge

Photo by T. Shade

Location: Use Connecticut Turnpike (I-95) Exits 51 (Eastbound) or 52 (Westbound), follow signs from East Haven Green to River St.

Ride: The Shore Line Trolley Museum operates the sole remaining segments of the historic, 87-year-old Branford Electric Railway. The 3-mile ride passes woods, salt marshes and meadows along the scenic Connecticut shore. Personally escorted tours of the carbarn and shop areas, given on every trip, allow passengers to view some of the 104 car collection of streetcars, interurbans and rapid transit equipment.

Schedule: Cars run Sundays, April thru December; Saturdays, May thru October. Open 11:00 A.M. to 5:00 P.M.

Fare: Unlimited rides and guided tour: Adults $3.50, Seniors $3.00, Children (2-11) $1.50, under 2 free. Rates and program may vary during Special Events Days. Reserved Group Discounts available.

Trolleys: Connecticut Co. open cars #1414 and #1425; Double-truck Jewett #193; Montreal double-truck #2001; Johnstown lightweight #356; Brooklyn, N.Y. convertible #4573; Lynchburg Rys. open car #34 and North Shore Interurban #709 are among the cars most often operated.

Special Events: National Trolley Festival/Railfan Day, October 10 & 11, 1987. Santa Claus Trolley Ride, first 3 week-ends in December.

Displays: Parlor Car #500, P.C.C. #1001 (first ever built), snow sweeper, interurbans, subway cars and work equipment on display or in the carbarns. The shop area displays many cars in various stages of rehabilitation. The Sprague Memorial Building houses photos, models, exhibits, a slide theater and a gift shop.

Shore Line Trolley Museum is a National Historic Site.

✔Refreshments
✔Gift Shop
✔Picnic Area
✔Memberships

Shore Line Trolley Museum
17 River Street
East Haven, CT 06512
Phone (203) 467-6927

 New Haven

CONNECTICUT, ESSEX
Valley Railroad Co.

The **Valley Railroad Company** *Connecticut Valley Line*

Steam, scheduled
Standard gauge

Photo © Howard Pincus

Location: Trains depart from depot at Essex, just west of Exit 3 of State Route 9. Valley Railroad is 4 miles north of the Connecticut Turnpike, use Exit 69 (Old Saybrook).

Ride: A 10-mile, 55-minute round trip over a former New Haven R.R. branch line. Take a nostalgic ride behind a steam locomotive through New England countryside to Chester, CT. At Deep River a connection is made with river boats for a scenic excursion on the Connecticut River.

Schedule: SPRING: May 2 thru June 7, Saturdays, Sundays & Memorial Day, 11:45 A.M., 1:15, 2:45, 4:15 P.M. Wednesdays at 2:00 & 3:30 P.M. June 10 thru June 25, Saturdays, Sundays, Wednesdays & Thursdays, 11:45 A.M., 1:15, 2:45, 4:15 P.M.

SUMMER: June 27 thru September 7, Daily operation. Trains at 10:30, 11:45 A.M., 1:15, 2:45, 4:15, *5:30 P.M. (*does not run week-days).

FALL: September 9 thru November 1, Daily except Mondays & Tuesdays, 11:45 A.M., 1:15, 2:45, 4:15 P.M. (Also runs Columbus Day). November 8 thru November 22, Sundays at 1:15 & 2:45 P.M. Also runs November 27.

WINTER: Christmas Trains operate November 28 thru December 27, on various dates. Consult railroad timetables for complete information.

Spring, Summer & Fall trains connect with riverboats for Connecticut River cruises. Amtrak connections at Old Saybrook.

Fare: Adults $6.95, Children (2-11) $2.95, under 2 free.
Additional charge for Riverboat. Groups of 25 or more, reduced rate.

Locomotives: #97, 2-8-0, Alco (1926), ex-Birmingham & Southeastern.
#40, 2-8-2, Alco (1920), ex-Aberdeen & Rockfish R.R.

Train: Open platform combination car, steel coaches. Pullman Parlor Car "Wallingford" (extra fare).

Displays: The Connecticut Valley Railroad Museum owns and displays a collection of railroad equipment on the grounds of the Valley Railroad. The C.V.R.M. is a non-profit, volunteer organization.

Locomotives: A number of diesel locomotives have been preserved by the Museum. These include an EMD E-9 passenger diesel recently painted in New York Central's original passenger paint scheme, an authentically painted New Haven RS-3 road-switcher and a Conrail road freight engine.

Rolling Stock: Former Sumter & Choctaw 2-6-2 #103 heads a train of vintage freight cars including rare flatcar, boxcar and tank car. Restored Maine Central baggage car #411 houses interpretive displays, restored Cotton Belt passenger caboose contains exhibits and sales counter.

Special Events: Railfan Day will be held on Saturday, November 7, 1987. This will be an all-day extravaganza of steam and diesel-powered passenger and freight trains. It will include photo run-bys, flea market and night photo sessions.

Museum: Connecticut Valley Railroad Museum, P.O. Box 97, Essex, CT 06426. Phone (tape-recording) (203) 767-0494.

Note: In addition to its regular schedule of passenger trains, Valley Railroad Co. operates a number of special trains. Included are Jazz Festival Trains, August 21, 22, 23, Murder Mystery Train, September 12 and Ghost Train, October 30. Contact Valley Railroad for complete details.
Send large SASE for colorful, free brochure and complete timetable.

Lynn Parrott, President

✔Refreshments
✔Gift Shop
✔Picnic Area
✔Free Parking

Valley Railroad Company
P.O. Box 452
Essex, CT 06426
Phone (203) 767-0103

 Old Saybrook

CONNECTICUT, WAREHOUSE POINT   **Electric, scheduled**
Connecticut Electric Railway Assn.   **Standard gauge**

Photo by Kenneth F. DeCelle

Location: The Museum is a few miles north of Hartford on Route 140. Take Bridge St. exit of Interstate 91 (Exit 45), go ½-mile east.

Ride: A 3-mile, 17-minute ride through scenic woodlands over a rebuilt portion of the old Rockville branch of the Hartford & Springfield Street Railway.

Schedule: Museum is open Saturdays, Sundays & Holidays, year-round (except Thanksgiving & Christmas Days). Cars operate Noon to 5:00 P.M.
Daily operation, May 25 through Labor Day. Cars operate 10:00 A.M. to 4:00 P.M. Winterfest, November 27-December 31 (except Dec. 24-25).

Fare: Adults $3.75, Children (5-15) $2.00, under 5 free.
Retired persons and group rates available.

Trolleys: #355, #840, #3001 from the Connecticut Co.;
#4, #2056, #2600 ex-Montreal Tramways; #1850 from Rio de Janeiro; #4436, #4284 ex-Chicago Transit Authority; #451, Illinois Terminal Ry.

Displays: Over 40 pieces of electric railway equipment are now at the Museum, with two more cars expected. The collection includes many streetcars, freight locomotives and work cars. Three steam locomotives may be seen: #5, 0-4-0T, Alco (Cooke), ex-Hartford Electric Light Co., a Climax from the Middle Fork R.R. and a fireless steam locomotive. Other railroad rolling stock includes an open platform passenger car, boxcars and caboose.

✔Gift Shop   Connecticut Electric Railway Assn., Inc.
✔Picnic Area   P.O. Box 360

TRAIN   East Windsor, CT 06088
Phone (203) 623-7417
(203) 623-2372 (Shop)

 Windsor Locks   (203) 627-6040 (Business Office)

DELAWARE, WILMINGTON
Wilmington & Western R.R.

Location: Trains leave from Greenbank Station located on Route 41, just north of Route 2, 4 miles southwest of Wilmington. From Exit 5 of I-95 take Rts. 141 or 41 north to Route 2, then Rt. 41 north.

Ride: An 8-mile, 1-hour round trip over a portion of the former B.&O.'s Landenberg Branch, from Greenbank Station to Mt. Cuba Picnic Grove. Every 4th Sunday, May thru October, 20-mile round trip operates to Hockessin crossing numerous bridges and trestles and 3 large rock cuts.

Schedule: Sundays, May thru October. Regular trains lv. at Noon, 1:15, 2:30 & 3:45 P.M. Every fourth Sunday trains lv. for Hockessin at Noon & 2:30 P.M. Many special trains, pre and post-season, Autumn Leaf, Christmas and other trips. Charter trips and group tours available.

Fare: To Mt. Cuba: Adults $5.00, Children (2-12) $3.00, under 2 free.
To Hockessin: Adults $9.00, Children (2-12) $5.00, under 2 free.

Locomotives: (Partial List): #3, 0-6-0T, Vulcan (1942), ex-U.S. Navy.
#37, 2-8-2T, Alco (1924), ex-Sugar Pine Lumber Co.
#98, 4-4-0, Alco (1909), ex-Mississippi Central.
D-3, S-2 diesel, Alco (1949), ex-Baltimore & Ohio #9115.
#4662, Rail-car, Brill (1925), ex-Pennsylvania R.R.
#8408, SW-1 diesel, E.M.D. (1942), ex-Baltimore & Ohio.

Train: Steel open-platform combine and coaches from Lackawanna, M.P. 54 coaches from Pennsylvania R.R.

Displays: Rotating locomotive displays along right-of-way. Historic railroad displays in 113-year-old station. This is the Wilmington & Western's 22nd year of operation. 1987 will mark the 115th year that trains have been operating on this line.

Donald W. Callender, Jr., Executive Director

✔Refreshments
✔Gift Shop
✔Picnic Area

Historic Red Clay Valley, Inc.
P.O. Box 5787
Wilmington, DE 19808
Phone (302) 998-1930

 Wilmington

Photo courtesy Smithsonian Institution

Location: Major railroad exhibits are housed in Railroad Hall in the National Museum of American History, 14th St. & Constitution Ave.

Displays: Railroad Hall is dominated by the Southern Railway's Pacific-type passenger locomotive, No. 1401. This huge engine stands by a large window. Other locomotives on exhibit include the Cumberland Valley's "Pioneer" built in 1851 and the "John Bull." There is a fine collection of scale models of locomotives and cars as well as a Seattle Cable Car of 1888. Adjacent to Railroad Hall are exhibits of other forms of transportation including motor vehicles and ships.

Admission: No charge.

Locomotives: #1401, 4-6-2, Alco (1926), Southern Railway.
"John Bull", 4-2-0, Stephenson (1831), Camden & Amboy R.R.
"Pioneer", 2-2-2, Wilmarth (1851).
"Jupiter", 4-4-0, Baldwin (1876), in Arts & Industries Bldg.
"Olomana", 0-4-2, Baldwin (1883), plantation locomotive.

Schedule: Open Daily, 10:00 A.M. to 5:30 P.M. except Christmas Day.

Note: Information leaflet No. 455, available on request, describes the railroad exhibits.

William L. Withuhn is Curator, Division of Transportation

✔Refreshments
✔Gift Shop
✔Restaurant

Smithsonian Institution
National Museum of American History
Washington, DC 20560

 Washington

Location: The Gold Coast Railroad Museum, at Metrozoo, is located one-half mile west of the S.W. 152nd St. exit of the Florida Turnpike, on the Metrozoo entrance road. Metrobus "Zoobus" provides public transportation connection with the Metrorail rapid transit at Dadeland North station.

Ride: A 2½-mile, 25-minute ride around the Museum site.

Schedule: Museum is open Saturdays, Sundays & Holidays, 10:00 A.M. to 5:00 P.M. Train ride operates every hour on the half-hour from 10:30 A.M. to 4:30 P.M.

Admission: Adults $4.25, Children (3-11) $2.25 tax included.

Locomotives: #153, 4-6-2, Alco (1922), ex-Florida East Coast Ry.
#113, 4-6-2, Alco (1913), ex-Florida East Coast Ry.
#167, SW-9 diesel, E.M.D. (1950), ex-Atlantic Coast Line.
#1555, RS-3 diesel, Alco (1955), ex-Long Island R.R.

Train: Coaches and Lackawanna commuter cars.

Displays: Famous Presidential Pullman car "Ferdinand Magellan", used by Presidents Roosevelt, Truman, Eisenhower and Reagan. California Zephyr dome-sleeper-lounge "Silver Crescent". Numerous other museum displays and rolling stock on display at the large train shed and depot area. The Gold Coast Railroad Museum is a non-profit organization.

✔Refreshments
✔Gift Shop
✔Memberships

Gold Coast Railroad Museum
12450 S.W. 152 Street
Miami, FL 33177
Phone (305) 253-0063

 Miami

Photo by Michael E. Cosgrove

Location: The Southeastern Railway Museum is located on U.S. 23 near Duluth, Ga., a short distance north of Atlanta.

Ride: The Atlanta Chapter sponsors steam and diesel powered excursion trains over lines of the Norfolk Southern. Please refer to the Norfolk Southern steam schedules for dates.

Schedule: Museum schedules: open Saturdays only (except on excursion dates) from 9:00 A.M. to 5:00 P.M.

Fare: Main-line excursions, determined by trip. For information and tickets, write Trip Chairman, P.O. Box 81592, Atlanta, GA 30366.

Locomotives: Main-line: #750, 4-6-2, Alco (1910), ex-Savannah & Atlanta Ry.; #290, 4-6-2, Lima (1926), ex-Atlanta & West Point. At museum: #97, 0-6-0T, Porter, ex-Georgia Power; #9, Heisler (1924), ex-Campbell Limestone Co.; #1100, SW-7 diesel, E.M.D. (1950), ex-Southern Ry.

Train: Main-line: Air-conditioned and open-air coaches, commissary car, open observation type cars.

Displays: Twelve-acre museum site at Duluth features steam and diesel locomotives, passenger and freight cars. Museum library, housed in ex-Southern R.P.O. #153, open by appointment.

Michael E. Cosgrove, President

✔Refreshments on train
✔Gift Shop on train
✔Memberships

Atlanta Chapter, N.R.H.S.
P.O. Box 13132
Atlanta, GA 30324
Phone (404) 476-2013

Amtrak ➤ Atlanta

Photo by James G. Bogle

Location: Train leaves from Zero Milepost near the Georgia Railroad Freight Depot at Underground Atlanta. Free parking at 90 Central Ave., adjacent to the Depot. The Depot is the oldest standing building in Atlanta, completed in 1869.

Ride: Regular trains leave from Zero Milepost, make an 18-mile, 1½-hour loop trip through Atlanta. Train travels through many historic areas of the City including the Martin Luther King Historic District, Inman Park, Chessie System piggyback yard and Emory University. Special trips to Stone Mountain Village take 2½-hours, connect with MARTA for access to Stone Mountain Park.

Schedule: Train operates Saturdays, departs Zero Milepost at 10:00 A.M., 12:00 & 2:00 P.M. on Loop Trip.
Stone Mtn. Village train runs on designated Saturdays, leaves 9:00 A.M., 12:00 & 3:00 P.M.

Fare: Adults $10.00, Children $5.00, under 3 free.

Locomotives: #750, 4-6-2, Alco (1910), ex-Savannah & Atlanta R.R.
#6901, E-8A passenger diesel, EMD (1951), ex-Southern Ry.

Train: Baggage car, coaches, dining car, observation car.

History: The Georgia Railroad was completed in September 1845 and ran from Augusta to the small village of Marthasville, later renamed "Atlanta". The Georgia Railroad's Freight Depot was built at Zero Milepost in what is now Atlanta.

Note: The train is operated by volunteers from the Atlanta Chapter of the National Railway Historical Society in cooperation with CSX Rail and Norfolk Southern Corporation.

✔Refreshments
✔Gift Shop
✔Free Parking

New Georgia Railroad
1 Martin Luther King, Jr. Drive
Atlanta, GA 30334
Phone (404) 656-3253

Amtrak ➤➤➤ Atlanta

55

Location: The depot is located in downtown Hartwell, 2 blocks from U.S. 29 on Jackson St. From Interstate 85, take the Hartwell exit, go 12 miles east. The site is in the northeast part of the state.

Ride: An 11-mile, 1-hour round trip from Hartwell to Air Line, GA. The line features sharp curves and grades as steep as 4%. Travel over the line of the Hartwell Railway, through pleasant farm lands and scenic countryside.

Schedule: Steam-powered passenger train will operate on major Holidays and on most Saturdays, May through October. Write for exact dates and times of departure. Diesel-powered charter trips by advance request. Dinner train by advance request.

Fare: Steam train: Adults $5.00, Children (4-11) $3.00.

Locomotives: #11, 2-6-2, Baldwin (1925), ex-Reader Railroad.
#2, 44-ton diesel, G.E. (1950), built for Hartwell Ry.
#5, 44-ton diesel, G.E. (1942), ex-N.Y.O.&W.Ry. #104.

Train: Former Lackawanna electric commuter coaches, Southern Railway 44-seat Dining Car, Central of Georgia caboose.

Displays: Pullman car, Office car, small museum in depot.

Craig A. Myers, General Manager

Hart County Scenic Ry.
P.O. Box 429
Hartwell, GA 30643
Phone (404) 376-2627

Location: Big Shanty Museum is located in Kennesaw, off Highways 41 & 75, about 25 miles north of Atlanta.

Displays: One of the most famous locomotives in American history is now enshrined in a museum building within 100 yards of the spot where it was stolen on April 12, 1862. The Andrews Raid and The Great Locomotive Chase was one of the unusual episodes of the Civil War and has been much publicized over the years. The locomotive "General" survived the war and has been displayed and exhibited many times. The old engine is operable and was last operated in 1962. The "General" was placed in the museum building at Kennesaw, formerly known as Big Shanty in 1972. The Big Shanty Museum was officially opened on April 12, 1972, 110 years after the historic seizure of the "General".

Schedule: Open Daily, 9:30 A.M. to 5:30 P.M. Sundays, Noon to 5:30 P.M. During December, January & February, hours are Noon to 5:30 P.M.

Admission: Adults $2.00, Children 50¢, under 8 free.

Locomotives: #3, 4-4-0, "General", Rogers, Ketchum & Grosvenor, Paterson, N.J. (1855), ex-Western & Atlantic R.R.

Exhibits: Diarama of the Lacy Hotel and the scene of the capture of April 12, 1862. The story of the chase and pictures of all the participants are also on display.

Carol McDonald, Manager

✔Gift Shop

Big Shanty Museum
2829 Cherokee St.
Kennesaw, GA 30144
Phone (404) 427-2117

GEORGIA, STONE MOUNTAIN
Stone Mountain Scenic Railroad

Steam, scheduled
Standard gauge

Location: The railroad is located within Georgia's Stone Mountain Park, 16 miles east of Atlanta. A new greatly enlarged station will open in 1987.

Ride: The line circles the base of famous Stone Mountain on a five-mile loop. Trip takes about 25 minutes.

Schedule: Steam trains operate Daily, year-round. Trains leave every 45 minutes from 10:00 A.M. to 5:00 P.M. From mid-June through mid-August, trains operate until 9:00 P.M.

Fare: Adults $2.50, Children $1.50, under 4 free. One-time admission to Park, $4.00.

Locomotives: #60, 4-4-0, Baldwin (1922), ex-Southern Pacific.
#104, 4-4-0, Baldwin (1919), ex-Red River & Gulf R.R.
#110, 2-6-2, Vulcan (1927), ex-Cliffside R.R.

Train: Ex-C.&N.W. coaches and combine resembling antebellum era cars. Also baggage car built over diesel locomotive to provide help for steam locos.

Displays: Stone Mountain is the largest solid mass of exposed granite on earth. A huge carving of Confederate heroes graces the steep north face of the mountain. The park also contains Campground, Inn, Beach, Waterslide, Golf, Tennis and six other major attractions.

✔Refreshments
✔Gift Shop
✔Picnic Area

Stone Mountain Scenic R.R.
P.O. Box 778
Stone Mountain, GA 30086
Phone (404) 498-5600

Amtrak➤ Atlanta

Location: The Sugar Cane Train runs from the resort areas of Puukolii and Kaanapali to the old whaling town of Lahaina on the island of Maui.

Ride: The L.K.&P. is an authentic replica of an old Hawaiian sugar cane railroad. Passengers take a 12-mile, 1-hour round trip from Kaanapali to the seaport town of Lahaina. The train winds through sugar cane fields, across a curved 400 ft. trestle and provides a spectacular view of the mountains and the neighboring islands.

Schedule: Operates Daily, year-round (except Thanksgiving and Christmas Days). Train makes five round trips a day from 9:35 A.M. to 4:10 P.M.

Fare: Round Trip: Adults $7.50, Children $3.75.
One Way: Adults $4.50, Children $2.25.

Locomotives: #1, "Anaka" 2-4-0, Porter (1943). #3, "Myrtle", 2-4-0, Porter (1943), both engines ex-Carbon Limestone Co.
#45, "Oahu 45" Plymouth diesel-mechanical, ex-Oahu Ry.

Train: Coaches are patterned after 1890 Kalakauan cars which ran on the Hawaiian Rail Road.

Gary Getman, General Manager

✔Refreshments
✔Gift Shop

L.K.&P. R.R.
P.O. Box 816
Lahaina, HI 96761
Phone (808) 661-0089

ILLINOIS, CHICAGO
Museum of Science & Industry

Museum, Railway Displays
Standard gauge

Location: Museum is located at 57th St. and Lake Shore Drive in Chicago.

Displays: One of the largest and finest museums in the country, Museum of Science & Industry devotes a great deal of its attention to transportation on land, sea and air. Notable exhibits include the German submarine U-505, a World War II British Spitfire aircraft, the Apollo 8 space module which orbited the moon and many, many other historic vehicles. The Santa Fe Miniature Railroad operates model trains over 1000 feet of trackage. There are many scale models of locomotives and trains.

Schedule: Open Daily. From Memorial Day through Labor Day, hours are 9:30 A.M. to 5:30 P.M. Rest of the year, closes at 4:00 P.M. on weekdays.

Admission: No charge.

Locomotives: #999, 4-4-0, West Albany Shops (1893), New York Central. The first steam locomotive to exceed 100 m.p.h., the famous #999 attained a speed of 112.5 m.p.h. west of Batavia, N. Y. in 1893. #2903, 4-8-4, Baldwin (1943), Santa Fe. This giant 304-ton locomotive was used in transcontinental passenger service until its retirement in July 1955. #9900, the Pioneer Zephyr, C.B.&Q. R.R. Built in 1934, this was the first streamlined diesel powered passenger train in the country.

✔Refreshments
✔Gift Shop
✔Restaurant

Museum of Science & Industry
57th St. & Lake Shore Drive
Chicago, IL 60637
Phone (312) 684-1414

Amtrak ▶ Chicago

ILLINOIS, MONTICELLO
Monticello Railway Museum

Steam, scheduled
Standard gauge

Location: The Museum is located near Exit 63 of I-72 in central Illinois. Monticello is about 20 miles southwest of Champaign and 30 miles northeast of Decatur.

Ride: A 4-mile, 40-minute round trip over former Illinois Terminal R.R. right-of-way. Trains depart from newly restored ex-I.C.G. depot.

Schedule: Saturdays, Sundays & Holidays only, Memorial Day week-end through Labor Day week-end. Trains depart at 1:00, 2:00, 3:00 & 4:00 P.M.

Fare: Adults $3.00, Children $1.75, 5 and under free with paid Adult fare. Includes museum displays and unlimited rides.

Locomotives: #1, 0-4-0, Alco (1930), ex-Montezuma Gravel Co.
#191, 0-6-0, Alco (1916), ex-Republic Steel Corp.
#401, 2-8-0, Baldwin (1907), ex-Southern.
#44, 44-ton diesel, Davenport (1940).
#3725, F-7A diesel, E.M.D. (1953), ex-Wabash #725.
#301, RS-3 diesel, Alco, ex-Long Island R.R.

Train: Combine, coaches, caboose.

Displays: Sleeper "Chief Illini", Shedd Aquarium Car "Nautilus" and ex-Nickel Plate Road Railway Post Office car.

✔Refreshments
✔Picnic Area
✔Gift Shop
✔Memberships

Monticello Railway Museum
Box 401
Monticello, IL 61856
Phone (217) 762-9011 during museum operating hours.

ILLINOIS, SOUTH ELGIN
Fox River Trolley Museum

Electric, scheduled
Standard gauge

Photo by Fred D. Lonnes

Location: South Elgin is located about 35 miles northwest of Chicago. The yard and depot are on Illinois Route 31, just south of I-90 and U.S. 20.

Ride: Trolleys operate on the Aurora, Elgin & Fox River Interurban Railway from Castlemuir (South Elgin) to Coleman and Coleman Grove (Blackhawk Forest Preserve). The nostalgic 3-mile, 30-minute trip runs immediately adjacent to the scenic Fox River.

Schedule: Sundays & Holidays, May 17 thru October 25, from 11:00 A.M. to 6:00 P.M.
Saturdays, June 27 thru August 29 from 1:00 to 5:00 P.M.

Fare: Adults, single-ride $2.00, Children $1.00. Inquire about 2-ride fares, 20/20 group rate and charter rates.

Trolleys: The oldest operating interurban car in America, Chicago, Aurora & Elgin #20, Niles (1902) and C.A.&E. interurban #316, Jewett (1913). Chicago, North Shore & Milwaukee #756, Standard (1930); Chicago Rapid Transit #4288, Cincinnati (1922) and #4451, Cincinnati (1924).

Displays: Additional trolley and railway equipment including Chicago Transit Authority steeple-cab locomotive #L-202, Chicago South Shops (1908); San Francisco PCC car #1030, St. Louis (1951); C.S.S.&S.B. combine #111 (1929); Chicago Rapid Transit #5001, Pullman (1947); Chicago Street Railway Post Office Car #6 (1895).

Special Events: ELECTRIC RAILROAD FAIR & Community Picnic, Saturday, June 27, 10:00 A.M. to 6:00 P.M.
WELCOME TO SUMMER, Sundays, June 7 & 14. AUTUMN COLOR, Sundays, October 4 & 11.

✔Refreshments
✔Gift Shop
✔Picnic Area

Fox River Trolley Museum
P.O. Box 315
South Elgin, IL 60177
Phone (312) 697-4676

ILLINOIS, UNION (MC HENRY COUNTY)
Illinois Railway Museum

Steam, Electric, Diesel
Standard gauge

Location: The Museum is on Olson Road, 1 mile east of Union.

Ride: A 4-mile, 20-minute round trip over the line of the former Elgin & Belvedere, featuring steam, electric and diesel operation.

Schedule: STEAM OPERATION: Saturdays & Sundays, May 16 thru September 27. Also runs May 25, August 1-9, July 3-4, September 7. Trains operate Noon to 5:00 P.M.
ELECTRIC OPERATION: Sundays, April 19 thru October 25; Saturdays, May thru September. Daily, Memorial Day thru Labor Day. Cars operate 10:00 A.M. to 4:00 P.M.

Fare: Admission to grounds, including unlimited rides: Adults $4.50, Children $2.25.

Locomotive Roster: #1630, 2-10-0, Baldwin (1918), ex-Frisco Lines.
#101, 2-6-2, Baldwin (1926), ex-Tuskegee R.R.
#5, 3-truck Shay, Lima (1929), ex-St. Regis Paper Co.
#8380, 0-8-0, Baldwin (1929), ex-Grand Trunk Western.
#265, 4-8-4, Alco (1944), ex-Milwaukee Road.
#16, 4-4-0, Baldwin (1915), ex-D.T.&I.R.R.
#2050, 2-8-8-2, Alco (1922), ex-Norfolk & Western Ry.
#3719, 2-6-0, Brooks (1900), ex-Illinois Central.
#3001, boxcab diesel, Ingersoll Rand (1926), ex-D.L.&W.
#760, H-10-44 diesel, Fairbanks-Morse (1944), ex-Milwaukee Road.
#9952-A, E-5 diesel, E.M.D. (1940), ex-Colorado & Southern.

Trolleys: North Shore, C.A.&E. & Illinois Terminal interurbans. Streetcars from Chicago and Milwaukee as well as Chicago "El" cars.

Displays: There are over 225 pieces of rail equipment on display at this extensive museum. The collection includes 18 steam locomotives, 19 diesels, a 5-car Burlington Zephyr train as well as numerous electric cars.

Special Events: Railfan Week-end will be held on Labor Day week-end, Fare $6.50. July 4, Trolley Pageant, September 26-27, Members' Days.

Nick Kallas, General Manager

✔Refreshments
✔Gift Shop
✔Picnic Area
✔Memberships

Illinois Railway Museum
P.O. Box 431
Union, IL 60180
Phone (815) 923-2488

INDIANA, ANGOLA
Little River Railroad

Photo by Charlie Willer

Location: Steam train leaves from depot at Pleasant Lake, 4½-miles south of the circle in Angola. The site is located near the junction of I-69 and the Indiana Toll Road. Take the Angola exit of I-69.

Ride: A 6-mile, 1-hour round trip over the line of the Hillsdale County Railway from Pleasant Lake to Steubenville and return. (Passengers may not board or alight at Steubenville).

Schedule: Steam train will operate on the following dates: May 23-25; June 21, 27-28; July 5, 25-26; Saturdays & Sundays in August; September 5-7, 20, 27; October 4, 11, 18, 1987. Trains leave Pleasant Lake at 1:00 & 2:00 P.M. (E.S.T.).

Fare: Adults $3.50, Children (5-11) $2.00. Charter trips available. Memberships, including one-year pass, $10.00 per year.

Locomotives: #110, 4-6-2, Baldwin (1911), ex-Little River R.R. This is the smallest standard gauge Pacific type locomotive ever built.

Train: Chicago & Alton combination car #2594, Milwaukee Road "Hiawatha" coaches, open-air cars, Baltimore & Ohio cabooses.

Note: A number of special events are planned for the 1987 season. In addition, train may make longer runs late in the season. Write for details.

✔Refreshments
✔Gift Shop
✔Picnic Area
✔Memberships

Little River Railroad
P.O. Box 178
Angola, IN 46703
Phone (219) 833-1804
(219) 825-9182

INDIANA, CONNERSVILLE
Whitewater Valley R.R.

Steam, scheduled
Standard gauge

Photo by Robert Sorg

Location: Trains leave from depot on State Route 121 in Connersville.

Ride: The 32-mile round trip on Indiana's longest and most scenic steam-powered railroad takes 5 hours, including a 2-hour layover at Metamora. The route runs along the old Whitewater Canal from Connersville to Metamora and return. At Metamora, a Caboose Train offers a half-hour, 4-mile round trip.

Schedule: Saturdays & Sundays, 1st week-end in May thru 1st week-end in November. Train departs Connersville starting at 11:30 A.M. (E.S.T.) Train also operates Memorial Day, July 4 and Labor Day. Christmas Rides operate Fridays, Saturdays & Sundays for 3 or 4 week-ends following Thanksgiving.

Fare: Connersville to Metamora, round trip: Adults $8.00, Children $4.00. One-way: Adults $7.00, Children $3.50. Christmas Rides, Adults $12.50, Children $6.25, advance paid reservations.

Locomotives: #100, 2-6-2, Baldwin (1919), ex-Florida Saw Mill Co. #6, 0-6-0, Baldwin (1907), ex-East Broad Top R.R. #25, diesel-electric switcher, Lima-Hamilton (1951), ex-Cincinnati Union Terminal. #210, G.E. diesel (1947); #9, Alco S-1 diesel (1947); gas switcher, Plymouth (1931).

Train: Coaches from Erie R.R., Rock Island, Baltimore & Ohio, Chicago & North Western. Baltimore & Ohio cabooses.

Displays: #3, 2-truck Heisler locomotive at Connersville. A museum at the Connersville depot contains displays of railroadiana.

Fred N. Bunzendahl, President

✔Refreshments
✔Gift Shop
✔Picnic lunches may be
   eaten aboard the train.
✔Memberships

TRAIN

Whitewater Valley R.R.
P.O. Box 406
Connersville, IN 47331
Phone (317) 825-2054

Photo by Grant Geist

Ride: Fort Wayne Railroad Historical Society operates day-long, main-line steam powered passenger excursions with its former Nickel Plate Berkshire locomotive.

Schedule: "The Wabash Cannon Ball" will operate between Fort Wayne and Peru, round-trip each day, September 13 & 14, 1987. Train leaves Norfolk & Western's East Wayne Terminal at 9:00 A.M., returns at 5:30 P.M. Train remains in Peru 4 hours.

Fare: Adults $39.00, Children (12 and under) $28.50.
All tickets are round-trip and include admission to the Circus at Peru. Ticket orders must be received by September 5. Please specify date and open-window or air-conditioned coach.

Locomotives: #765, 2-8-4, Lima (1944), ex-Nickel Plate Road. This Class S-2 Berkshire is maintained and operated by the organization.

Train: Main-line coaches, both air-conditioned cars and open-window cars. Pullman Cars, dome car, lounge car may be added to train.

Other Trips: Other trips may be operated during the year, please write to the address below for details.

Note: Mail orders for tickets should be sent to the following address: Ticket Agent, F.W.R.H.S., Box 535, New Haven, IN 46774. Credit card orders may be phoned to (219) 749-9002.

✔Refreshments on train
✔Gift Shop on train
✔Memberships

 Fort Wayne

Fort Wayne Railroad Historical Society
P.O. Box 11017
Fort Wayne, IN 46855

INDIANA, FRENCH LICK
French Lick, West Baden & Southern Ry.

Steam, Electric, scheduled
Standard gauge

Photo by Cecil J. Smith, Jr.

Location: Trains depart from the old Monon R.R. passenger station in French Lick. The site is located on State Route 56 in the southwest part of the State, about an hour's drive from Louisville.

Ride: A 20-mile, 1¾-hour round trip between the resort town of French Lick and Cuzco, site of Patoka Lake. The train traverses wooded Indiana limestone country and passes through one of the state's longest railroad tunnels. Trolley makes a 2-mile trip from French Lick to West Baden and return.

Schedule: Trains operate Saturdays & Sundays April 4 thru November 29, plus Memorial Day and Labor Day. Trains depart at 10:00 A.M., 1:00 & 4:00 P.M., E.S.T.
Trolley operates Daily, May thru October and week-ends in April and November. Departs every half-hour from 10:00 A.M. to 4:00 P.M.

Fare: Steam Train: Adults $6.00, Children (3-11) $3.00, under 3 free.
Trolley: $1.00 per person, under 3 free.

Locomotives: #208, 2-6-0, Baldwin (1912), ex-Angelina & Neches River R.R.
#97, 2-6-0, Baldwin (1925), ex-Mobile & Gulf R.R.
#3, 80-ton diesel, G.E. (1947).
#1, S-4 diesel, Alco, ex-Algers, Winslow & Western Ry.

Trolleys: #313, Porto, Portugal streetcar (1930).

Train: Erie and Rock Island coaches, Erie snack-bar car.

Displays: The French Lick, West Baden & Southern Ry. is operated by the Indiana Railway Museum. The group owns 57 pieces of railway equipment.

G. Alan Barnett, President & General Manager

✔Refreshments
✔Gift Shop
✔Memberships

French Lick, West Baden & Southern Ry.
P.O. Box 150
French Lick, IN 47432

INDIANA, HESSTON
Operating Steam Museum

Steam, scheduled
Various gauges

Photo by Edward Rysz

Location: Take Indiana Toll Road to Exit 7. Turn north on Ind. 39 approximately 6½ miles to County Road 1000N. Turn right 2½ miles to grounds or take I-94 to Exit 1 at New Buffalo, Mich. Turn south 2 miles to County Road 1000N. Turn left 2½ miles to grounds.

Ride: A 2-mile, 15-minute trip over unique dual-gauge (24" & 36") trackage through the 155 acre grounds of the LaPorte County Historical Steam Society. Also ride the 1½" scale, steam-powered train over a 5000 ft. loop, and a ¼" scale steam train over a 5000 ft. loop of track.

Schedule: Week-ends, Memorial Day through Labor Day. Sundays only, Labor Day through October. Trains operate 1:00 to 6:00 P.M. Annual Steam Show held Labor Day Week-end.

Fare: Adults $2.00, Children $1.50.

Locomotives: #2, 2-6-0, Porter (1911), ex-United Fruit, Guatemala (3 ft.) #1, 0-4-0T, Henschel (1935), Germany (2 ft.) #7, 3-truck Shay, Lima (1929), ex-New Mexico Lumber Co. (3 ft.).
#19-B, 0-4-0T, Sharp & Stewart (Glasgow, Scotland), (1889), ex-Darjeeling & Himalayan Ry. (2 ft.) pictured above, restored and in use. Four additional 2 ft. gauge steam locomotives will be added to the collection during 1987.

Train: Open excursion-type cars.

Displays: In addition to the rare and unusual steam locomotives operating here is a large collection of steam-powered equipment. Featured is a 350 h.p. Allis-Chalmers Corliss steam engine, steam traction engines, water pumps, sawmill, electric light plant and antique gas engines and tractors.

✓Gift Shop
✓Memberships

LaPorte County Historical Steam Society
2940 Mt. Claire Way
Michigan City, IN 46360
Phone (219) 778-2783

68

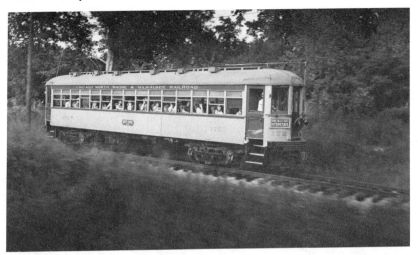

Location: The Indiana Transportation Museum is located at Forest Park, on State Route 19, about 20 miles north of Indianapolis.

Ride: A 2-mile, 20-minute ride in vintage electric interurban cars running through the museum site.

Schedule: Week-ends and Holidays (weather permitting), from March through mid-December. Hours of operation are Noon to 5:00 P.M. or dusk.

Fare: Adults $3.00, Children (6-12) $2.00, Family $8.00.

Locomotives: #587, 2-8-2, Baldwin (1918), ex-Nickel Plate Road. This locomotive, which was on display in Broad Ripple Park, Indianapolis for many years, is being restored for operation. Restoration should be completed during 1987 and there is a possibility of steam excursions later in the year.

Trolleys: #172, CNS&M interurban coach; #4293 & #4454, CRT cars; #4, Twin Branch R.R. electric locomotive; #1, Singer engine (1898).

Train: Excursions for 1987 to be announced. Train consists of F-7 diesel and a variety of passenger cars. Call for information.

Displays: Transportation and communications exhibits change seasonally. New York Central 20th Century Limited observation car "Sandy Creek", Louisville & Nashville dining car "Cross Keys Tavern", Henry M. Flagler's Business Car #90 from Florida East Coast Ry. Many other cars and equipment.

✓Refreshments
✓Gift Shop
✓Picnic Area in Park
✓Camping in Park
✓Memberships

TRAIN

Indiana Transportation Museum
P.O. Box 83
Noblesville, IN 46060
Phone (317) 773-6000

Amtrak Indianapolis

Photo by George Eckstein

Location: Boone is located in central Iowa, about 35 miles north of Des Moines. Passengers board trains at 10th & Division Sts. in Boone.

Ride: An 11-mile, 1½-hour round trip over the route of the former Fort Dodge, Des Moines & Southern R.R., once Iowa's longest electric interurban railroad. The train passes over a 156 ft. high bridge in the scenic Des Moines River valley.

Schedule: Trains operate Daily from Memorial Day week-end until the end of October. Departs week-days at 1:30 P.M., Saturdays, Sundays & Holidays at 11:00 A.M., 1:30 & 4:00 P.M. Group charters available.

Fare: Adults $6.00, Children $3.00, in arms free.

Locomotives: #7858, 80-ton diesel, G.E. (1943), ex-U.S.Air Force.
#1003, NW-2 diesel, E.M.D., ex-Chicago & North Western.
#475, 4-8-0, Baldwin (1906), ex-Norfolk & Western Ry.
#17, 2-8-0, Canadian (1940), ex-Crab Orchard & Egyptian.

Train: CSS&SB electric cars as trailers, Rock Island commuter coach, open observation cars, restored Northern Pacific 1902 wooden bay-window caboose.

Displays: The Iowa Railway Museum is housed in the new Boone & Scenic Valley depot. There are display tracks with a growing collection of rail equipment. Electric operations will begin in the yard area during 1987. Boone is the home of the Chicago & North Western's Central Division and the Kate Shelley high bridge, the longest double-track railroad bridge in the world.

✔Refreshments
✔Gift Shop
✔Picnic Area
✔Memberships

Boone & Scenic Valley R.R.
P.O. Box 603
Boone, IA 50036
Phone (515) 432-4249

Photo by Leo R. Clark

Location: Mt. Pleasant, in south-eastern Iowa, is the site of the yearly Midwest Old Settlers & Threshers Reunion.

Ride: A steam train ride through the grounds of the Midwest Old Settlers & Threshers Reunion. The Reunion, held on September 3-7, 1987, is a leading event of its type and features a large display of steam-powered farm equipment, antique cars and an old midwest farm village.

Schedule: September 3 through 7, 1987 during the Reunion. Two trains in operation, service every 10 minutes.

Fare: Adults $1.50, Children 75¢.
Admission to grounds, $6.00 for all 5 days.

Locomotives: #2, 2-6-0, Baldwin (1906), ex-Argent Lumber Co.
#6, 2-6-0, Baldwin (1891), ex-Argent Lumber Co.
#9, 3-truck Shay, Lima (1923), ex-West Side Lumber Co.

Train: Six wooden, open-platform coaches and caboose.

Displays: Model A fire car from West Side Lumber Co., a Fairmont track car and a hand-pump car can also be seen. The public is invited to tour our shops.

Note: The Midwest Central Railroad is a non-profit, educational organization.

✔Refreshments
✔Gift Shop
✔Picnic Area
✔Restaurant
✔Trailer Parking

Midwest Central Railroad
Box 102-H
Mt. Pleasant, IA 52641
Phone (319) 385-2912

 Mt. Pleasant

IOWA, MT. PLEASANT
Midwest Electric Railway

Electric, irregular
Standard gauge

Photo by Tom Konieczny

Ride: Trolleys provide transportation to a 60-acre campground during the Midwest Old Settlers & Threshers Annual Reunion. Non-camping visitors can ride from the exhibition grounds to Log Village and return on a 1½-mile loop track. Over 47,000 visitors were transported during the 1986 Reunion.

Schedule: Cars operate during the Reunion, September 3 to 7, 1987, from 7:00 A.M. to midnight, on a 3-minute headway.

Fare: Adults, Children, 75¢ round-trip, 40¢ one-way. Multi-ride discount available. Admission to Reunion: $6.00 for all five days.

Trolleys: #1718, 72 passenger open bench car, built 1920.
#1779, 65 passenger open bench car, built 1911.
(Both above cars from Rio de Janeiro, Brazil).
#9, combination car, built 1915 by the Southern Iowa R.R.
#320, Chicago, Aurora & Elgin wooden interurban car, built by Jewett Car Co. in 1914.
#381, Waterloo, Cedar Falls & Northern Master Unit, built 1930. This was the last streetcar to operate in regular service in Iowa.
#4476, P.C.C. car from Toronto Transit Commission, built by St. Louis Car Co. and Canadian Car Co. in 1949.

Displays: The Annual Reunion of the Midwest Old Settlers and Threshers Assn., with its 170 acres of showground, includes over 100 steam traction engines, tractors, gas engines, Corliss stationary engines, crafts, villages and antiques. It is always held for five days each year, ending Labor Day.

The Midwest Electric Railway, a subsidiary of the Midwest Old Settlers and Threshers Assn., is a volunteer organization.

✔Refreshments
✔Gift Shop
✔Picnic Area
✔Restaurants
✔Campgrounds

Midwest Electric Railway
R.R. #1
Mt. Pleasant, IA 52641

 Mt. Pleasant

KENTUCKY, LOUISVILLE
Kentucky Railway Museum

Railway Museum
Standard gauge

Photo by Thomas R. Schultz

Location: Kentucky Railway Museum's Ormsby Station is east of Louisville on Lagrange Road at Dorsey Lane. Leave I-264 at U.S. 60 East, turn left on S.R. 146 for 3.3 miles.

Ride: A 2-mile, 20-minute diesel-powered ride through the grounds of the Museum over former L.A. & P.V. right-of-way.

Schedule: The Museum is open Saturdays, Sundays & Holidays, May through October. Open Daily, except Monday, during June, July & August. Hours are 11:00 A.M. to 5:00 P.M., except Sundays 12:30 to 5:30 P.M.

Admission: Adults $2.00, Seniors $1.50, Children $1.50, under 5 free. Special rates for group tours.

Locomotives: Newly restored steam locomotive #152, 4-6-2, Rogers (1905), ex-Louisville & Nashville R.R. will operate over Museum trackage on July 4th week-end and Labor Day week-end.

Displays: On exhibit is a wide variety of railway rolling-stock from area rail lines. Monon model BL-2 #32 and Alco diesel switcher #7374 are operable as is L.&N. steam wrecker #40010. Equipment on display includes 2 Southern Ry. coaches, 2 Milwaukee Road "Hiawatha" coaches, L.&N. Pullman-Lounge "Mt. Broderick", L.&N. sleeper "Pearl River", L.&N. combine #1603, an Illinois Central caboose and other passenger and freight equipment. Also an 1873 Louisville mule-drawn streetcar and an ex-Southern Pacific Dining Car.

✔Gift Shop
✔Memberships

Kentucky Railway Museum
P.O. Box 22764
Louisville, KY 40222-0764
Phone (502) 245-6035

Photo by Emmet Blum

Location: The Museum is located at 519 Williams Blvd. in Kenner. The site is just off Interstate 10 near the New Orleans International Airport. The main-line of the Illinois Central Gulf R.R. is next to the Museum building.

Displays: On display in the Museum are operating N, HO and O scale model railroad lay-outs. There is also a Cagney 4-4-0 15" gauge live-steam locomotive, a 4-4-0 9" gauge live-steamer and a 15" gauge four-wheeled gasoline plantation locomotive. Also a full-size mock-up of a New Orleans Public Service streetcar vestibule, where visitors can play at being Motorman. There is an extensive collection of railroad china and tableware as well as a library and numerous railroad artifacts.

Schedule: Tuesdays through Saturdays, year-round, 9:00 A.M. to 5:00 P.M., Sundays, 1:00 to 5:00 P.M.

Admission: Adults $1.00, Children 50¢.

Train Ride: 15" gauge train at nearby Kenner City Park operates week-ends, weather permitting. Adults $1.00, Children 50¢.

Rolling Stock: #745, 2-8-2, T.&N.O. Algiers Shops (1921), ex-Southern Pacific. A.&W.P. wreck train with 115-ton steam wrecker, tender and work cars. RS-1 diesel #9969, ex-Rock Island. Southern heavyweight coach "Sea Island", Southern heavyweight Pullman "Glacier". Frisco diner #2, A.C.L. coaches #1055 & 1056 and S.P. bay-window caboose. Also tank car PPGX 121, New Orleans S.&W.B. boxcab electric and Porter compressed air locomotive.

Note: The Louisiana State Railroad Museum is the official state railroad museum and is operated by the Old Kenner Railway Assn. and the Pontchartrain Chapter of the National Railway Historical Society.

Jack A. Kasdan, President

✔Refreshments
✔Gift Shop
✔Memberships

Louisiana State Railroad Museum
P.O. Box 1835
Kenner, LA 70063
Phone (504) 468-7223

 New Orleans

Photo by John E. Helbok

Location: Boothbay Railway Village is located 8 miles from U.S. Route 1, on State Route 27 in Boothbay.

Ride: A 1½-mile, 15-minute trip through woods, through a covered bridge and past many railroad structures. The 2 ft. gauge railroad is reminiscent of the many slim-gauge lines which formerly ran in the State.

Schedule: Daily, mid-June through mid-September, then Week-ends through Columbus Day. Trains depart every half-hour, 9:30 A.M. to 5:00 P.M.

Fare: Adults $4.00, Children $2.00, under 2 free.
Group rates available.

Locomotives: #12313, 0-4-0T, Henschel (1913), ex-City of Hamburg; #22486, 0-4-0T, Henschel (1934); #24022, 0-4-0T, Henschel (1938); #24023, 0-4-0T, Henschel (1938); #10187, 0-4-0T, Baldwin (1895); #10188, 0-4-0T, Baldwin (1895).

Train: Closed coach, open coach and caboose.

Rolling Stock: Two-foot gauge equipment includes Sandy River & Rangeley Lakes combination car #11 (ex-Franklin & Meganic #1); S.R.&R.L. box cars #143 & #147; Wiscasset & Quebec box car #34 and W.W.&F. handcar. Standard gauge Maine Central caboose.

Displays: Village complex includes a restored railroad station, expanded antique auto and truck display and narrow-gauge photographic exhibit. Also a firehouse and more than 27 buildings in the village.

✔Refreshments
✔Gift Shop
✔Picnic Area
✔Memberships

Boothbay Railway Village
P.O. Box 123
Boothbay, ME 04537
Phone (207) 633-4727

MAINE, KENNEBUNKPORT
New England Electric Ry. Historical Society, Inc.
Seashore Trolley Museum

Electric, scheduled

Standard gauge

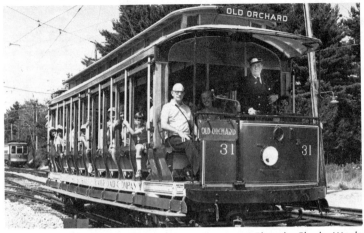

Photo by Charles Woolnough

Location: Seashore Trolley Museum is located on Log Cabin Road, off U.S. 1, 3 miles north of Kennebunk. The site is about 20 miles south of Portland and a short distance from the Maine Turnpike.

Ride: Along the former Atlantic Shore Line interurban right-of-way for a 2½-mile, 20-minute round trip and a ⅓-mile ride to the exhibit area. Different cars are used in rotation to demonstrate the equipment.

Schedule: Open Daily from April 25 through October 18. Hours of operation: Spring and Fall at 1:30 P.M. sharp. Week-ends and Labor Day week, May 23-June 14 and September 8-October 25, Noon to 5:00 P.M. Daily operation, June 20 through September 7, 10:00 A.M. to 5:30 P.M.

Fare: Adults $3.50, Seniors $3.00, Children $2.00, Family $11.00. Admission charge covers regularly scheduled rides and all exhibits.

Trolleys: The 172 cars in the collection include 74 city cars, 16 interurban cars, 8 rapid transit cars, 8 trackless trolleys, 9 buses, 4 plows and sweepers, 18 work cars, 6 mail and express cars, 5 locomotives, 15 railroad freight cars and 9 miscellaneous vehicles. Some of the collection, not currently on display, is not accessible. During the year, some 40 different cars will be used. On any one day, 2 to 6 cars will be demonstrated.

Displays: Seashore Trolley Museum is the oldest and largest electric railway collection in the country. A selection of cars is on display in two carbarns. Cars in one barn are open and lighted for visitors to see.

Special Events: June 21, Old Time Trolley Day; July 5, Canada Day; July 19, Yankee Trolley Day; October 31, Interurban to the Loop; December 5-6, Christmas Program.

✔Refreshments
✔Gift Shop
✔Picnic Area
✔Memberships

Seashore Trolley Museum
Drawer A
Kennebunkport, ME 04046
Phone: (207) 967-2712

Location: The B.&O. Railroad Museum is located in a century-old circular roundhouse and two adjacent historic structures. Mt. Clare Station, the nation's first railroad depot, is the entrance to this superb museum. Located at Pratt & Poppleton Streets, the site is a short distance from downtown Baltimore's famous Inner Harbor.

Displays: On display is the world-famous collection of historic locomotives and cars preserved by the Baltimore & Ohio R.R. Under the auspices of the Chessie System, the collection has been augmented by a number of Chesapeake & Ohio and Western Maryland locomotives. Outdoor display tracks accommodate large exhibits including steam, diesel and electric locomotives, passenger and freight cars.

Locomotives: This is the country's most comprehensive collection of locomotives. Some of the engines on display include the "William Mason", a beautiful 4-4-0 built in 1856; a B.&O. President series Pacific; Jersey Central "Camelback" #552 and streamlined C.&O. Hudson #490. A huge "Little Joe" electric freight engine, a P.R.R. GG-1 electric passenger engine and numerous vintage diesels are on display.

Schedule: Open Wednesday through Sunday, 10:00 A.M. to 4:00 P.M. year-round. Closed Mondays, Tuesdays and National Holidays.

Admission: Adults $2.50, Children (6-12) $1.50, under 6 free.
Group rates available.

✔Gift Shop
"Mt. Clare Shop"
✔Snack service

The B.&O. Railroad Museum
Pratt & Poppleton Sts.
Baltimore, MD 21223
Phone (301) 237-2387/2381

Amtrak ➤ Baltimore

MARYLAND, BALTIMORE
Baltimore Streetcar Museum

Electric, scheduled
5 ft. 4½" gauge

Location: The Baltimore Streetcar Museum is located at the former terminal of the Maryland & Pennsylvania R.R. at 1901 Falls Road. The site is 3-4 blocks from the Amtrak (P.R.R.) station.

Ride: A streetcar leaves the carhouse every fifteen minutes for a 1¼-mile round trip alongside Falls Road.

Schedule: Cars operate every Sunday, year-round, from Noon to 5:00 P.M. Also operates Saturdays, June through October plus Memorial Day, Independence Day and Labor Day, Noon to 5:00 P.M.

Fare: Adults $1.00, Children (4-11) 50¢. All day pass, $3.00.

Trolleys: #554, Single-truck summer car, Brownell Car Co. (1896). #264, Convertible car, Brownell Car Co. (1900). #1164, Double-truck summer car, J. G. Brill Co. (1902). #3828, Double-truck closed car, J. G. Brill Co. (1902). #7407, P.C.C. car, Pullman-Standard (1944).

Displays: A total of 13 cars (11 electric and 2 horsecars) tracing street rail transit in Baltimore from 1860 to 1963 are housed in a modern carbarn. A Visitors Center houses additional displays including an audio-visual presentation, "Rails Into Yesterday."

✔Refreshments
✔Gift Shop
✔Memberships

Amtrak▶━━ Baltimore

Baltimore Streetcar Museum, Inc.
P.O. Box 4881
Baltimore, MD 21211
Phone (301) 547-0264

Location: The Ellicott City B.&O. R.R. Station Museum is located at Maryland Ave. & Main St. in Ellicott City. The site is 4½ miles west of the Baltimore Beltway (I-695), use Exit 13.

Displays: Built in 1831, this stone station is the oldest surviving railroad station in America. It is a Registered National Historic Landmark. Visitors may receive a tour of the restored building, including a sight and sound show "The Greatest Railroad Adventure" which depicts the beginning of railroading in America. An HO gauge model railroad layout of the 13 miles from Baltimore to Ellicott City in the 1870's is housed in the restored 1885 freight house.

Schedule: Mid-January through March, open Saturdays & Sundays. April through mid-January, open Wednesdays through Sundays. Also open Mondays during July and August. Hours are from 11:00 A.M. (Noon on Sundays) to 4:00 or 5:00 P.M. depending on the day.

Admission: Adults $2.00, Seniors $1.50, Children (5-12) $1.00, under 5 free. Group rates available. Birthday parties accommodated in a restored 1927 Baltimore & Ohio caboose adjacent to the Museum.

Jack Mitchell, Museum Director

✔Gift Shop

Amtrak ➤➤➤ Baltimore

Ellicott City B.&O. R.R. Station Museum
P.O. Box 244
Ellicott City, MD 21043
Phone (301) 461-1944

MARYLAND, UNION BRIDGE
Maryland Midland Ry.

Diesel, scheduled
Standard gauge

Location: This short-line common-carrier railroad operates over lines once a part of both the Western Maryland Ry. and the Pennsylvania R.R. in the western part of Maryland. The Western Maryland portion of the line up the Catoctin Mountains features steep grades, sharp curves, high bridges and is an extremely scenic rail trip.

Ride: Passenger trains operate from Union Bridge over a former Western Maryland Ry. line, and also from Taneytown over a former Pennsylvania R.R. line.

Schedule: Union Bridge to Rocky Ridge on June 7, July 19, August 16, September 13, October 4, November 8.
Union Bridge to Highfield on June 13, July 11, August 8, October 3 & 24-25, November 7.
Union Bridge to Westminster on September 5 & 7.
Union Bridge to Thurmont on October 17 & 31.
Taneytown to Keymar : to be announced.

Fare: Varies with trip.

Locomotives: E.M.D. FP-7, GP-9 and SD-24 diesels, 65-ton Whitcomb.

Train: Lightweight air-conditioned coaches, open-window coach, dome dining car. Heavyweight business car (when First Class fares are offered).

Note: Trains depart from the following locations:
Union Bridge — Station on North Main St., MD-75.
Taneytown — Baltimore St.

✔Refreshments on train
✔Gift Shop
✔Brochure available

Maryland Midland Railway
P.O. Box A
Union Bridge, MD 21791
Phone (301) 775-2520

Photo by John J. Hilton

Location: On Bonifant Road between Layhill Road and New Hampshire Ave. north of Wheaton, Md.

Ride: The National Capital Trolley Museum operates over a one-mile right-of-way through the Northwest Branch Park. The 2-mile round trip takes about 20 minutes. Trolleys are boarded at a visitors' center built to resemble an old-time railroad station.

Schedule: Trolleys operate year-round. Saturdays and Sundays, Noon to 5:00 P.M. Also Memorial Day, July 4 and Labor Day. During July and August cars will also operate Wednesdays, Noon to 4:00 P.M. Closed December 15 through January 1.

Fare: Adults $1.00, under 18 years 75¢, under 2 free.

Trolleys: #678, New York & Vienna. #120, Graz, Austria. #955, Dusseldorf, Germany. #5954, Berlin, Germany. #6062 & Trailer, Vienna, Austria. #352, Johnstown, Pa. #522, #766, #1053, #1101, sweepers #07 & #026, work car #0509, Washington, D.C.

Displays: Slide show: "Washington's Trolleys Revisited" and exhibit hall. An "O" Gauge trolley layout is in operation.

✔Museum Shop
✔Memberships

 Washington
Silver Spring

National Capital Trolley Museum
P.O. Box 4007, Colesville Branch
Silver Spring, MD 20904
Phone (301) 384-9797
(301) 384-6088

81

MASSACHUSETTS, HYANNIS
Cape Cod & Hyannis R.R.

Diesel, scheduled
Standard gauge

Location: Trains depart from Boston area (Braintree Red Line subway station), Brockton, Bridgewater, Middleboro, Wareham, Buzzards Bay, Sandwich, West Barnstable and Hyannis.

Ride: Daily rail service operates between Greater Boston and Cape Cod. Daytrips to Sandwich, Hyannis or Martha's Vineyard available, Up to five trips per day. Train passes over famous vertical lift railroad bridge at Cape Cod Canal. Many local Cape Cod excursions from Hyannis, Buzzards Bay and Sandwich Village depots. Travel through cranberry bogs, sand dunes, salt marshes on a round-trip or connect with Canal Cruise or Martha's Vineyard boats. New this year is a Dinner Train.

Schedule: Daily operation from May 23 through October 18, 1987. Up to five trips per day. Call or write for complete timetables and information.

Fare: Varies with trip. Adults range from $9.00 to $23.00. Lesser children's fare.

Locomotives: #1202, #1210, GP-9 diesels, formerly New Haven Railroad.

Train: Coaches from Jersey Central and Canadian National R.R.'s, Pullman parlor car, tavern car, 1912 dining car.

Note: Bicycles carried for nominal fee. Group fares and private charters available.

✔Refreshments
✔Gift Shop

 Boston

Cape Cod & Hyannis R.R.
252 Main Street
Hyannis, MA 02601
Phone (617) 771-1145

Photo by Jack Armstrong

Location: Train departs from Sullivan Station in Lee, at the end of Canal St., off U.S. Route 20. One-mile north of Exit 2 (Lee) of Massachusetts Turnpike.

Ride: A 30-mile, 2½-hour round trip from Lee to Great Barrington, stopping at Norman Rockwell's town of Stockbridge with a flagstop at Housatonic. Train crosses the Housatonic River three times. Narration is provided. Passengers may leave the early train and reboard the later train for the return trip.

Schedule: Train leaves Lee Saturdays, Sundays & Holidays, Memorial Day week-end through October, departs at 10:30 A.M. and 2:00 P.M. "Cabaret Special" runs Fridays during July and August at 6:00 P.M., features live entertainment.

Fare: Adults $7.00, Seniors $6.00, Children (5 - 12) $4.00, under 5 free.

Locomotives: #19, 80-ton diesel, G.E. (1947), ex-General Electric Corp. #8619, SW-8 diesel, E.M.D. (1953), ex-New York Central R.R. 50-ton diesel, G.E. (1957), ex-United Illuminating.

Train: 5 ex-Erie-Lackawanna commuter coaches built in 1924.

Displays: Pennsylvania R.R. P-70 museum coach, model railroad, cabooses.

Special Events: Train robberies, Independence Day "Americana Special", Lee Sale-bration, Halloween Party.

✔Refreshments
✔Gift Shop

Berkshire Scenic Railway
P.O. Box 298
Lee, MA 01238
Phone (413) 243-2872

MASSACHUSETTS, LOWELL
Lowell Park Trolley

Photo by James Higgins

Location: The Lowell National Historical Park complex encompasses a canal system, large mill buildings and 19th century commercial buildings. The Lowell Park Trolley was created to move visitors within the Park, serving as both historical exhibits and active public transportation.

Ride: The Trolley runs on one mile of Boston & Maine R.R. track which links the historic downtown mill complexes with the canal barge system. Rides included in Park tours or the cars may be boarded at the Mack Building site.

Schedule: Cars #1601 & #1602 run Daily, Memorial Day week-end through Columbus Day. Cars operate continuously, 9:00 A.M. to 5:00 P.M. Closed car #1431 will run year-round, schedule to be announced.

Fare: No charge.

Trolleys: #1601 & #1602, authentic reproductions of the 1600-series cars built in 1901 by the J.G. Brill Co. for the Eastern Massachusetts Street Railway. These double-truck open cars were built in 1983. Closed streetcar #1431 is a replica of a 4100-series car built in 1912 for the Bay State Street Railway. These are the first new trolley cars to be built in the United States for over 50 years. The cars were built by the GOMACO Corp. of Ida Grove, Iowa.

Note: Lowell National Historical Park was established in 1978 and is a part of the National Park Service, U.S. Dept. of Interior. Reservations are required for the various Park tours which are offered.

✔Refreshments
✔Gift Shop

MBTA - Lowell

Lowell National Historical Park
169 Merrimack Street
Lowell, MA 01852
Phone (617) 459-1000

Location: A.&D. Toy Train Village is located at 49 Plymouth St. in Middleboro, 2 miles north of the Middleboro rotary, at the junction of Rts. 18, 28, 44 and I-495. The site is a short distance from the Edaville Railroad, near Cape Cod.

Displays: Literally thousands of toy trains of every size and every era are shown in this museum. There are 50 operating lay-outs in all gauges from tiny Z Gauge to large Standard Gauge. There is a 6-level master lay-out in operation. There are 35 permanent exhibits showing over 2000 trains made from 1850 through the present, from 21 different countries. Many pushbuttons allow visitors to operate various trains. This large, diversified toy train museum first opened in 1984. Allow at least 1 hour for your visit.

Schedule: Museum is open Daily year-round (except Thanksgiving, Christmas & New Year's Day from 10:00 A.M. to 5:00 P.M. Toy Train Christmas Festival held from mid-November through first week of January.

Admission: Adults $3.00, Seniors $2.50, Children (5-12) $1.50, under 5 free. All Railroad pass-holders receive 20% discount on admissions.
Access for handicapped. Baby-changing station. Air-conditioned.

Note: Numerous special events will be held during 1987. Call or write for free calendar of events. Memberships are available which include unlimited pass, newsletter and other benefits such as access to large research library. Unique Gift Shop has over 250 train-related gifts.

Adolf W. Arnold, Founder and Curator

✔Gift Shop
✔Free Parking
✔Memberships

A.&D. Toy Train Village
49 Plymouth St.
Middleboro, MA 02346
Phone (617) 947-5303

Photo by Edwill H. Brown

Ride: A 5½-mile, 30-minute ride through the cranberry bogs near Cape Cod. Edaville R.R. operates vintage locomotives and cars from the once extensive network of Maine 2-foot gauge railroads.

Schedule: Week-ends in May, Noon to 5:00 P.M.
Daily operation, June thru Labor Day, 10:00 A.M. to 5:30 P.M.
September 7 thru October 25, Week-ends & Holidays, 10:00 A.M. to 5:30 P.M. with Steam; Week-days 10:00 A.M. to 3:00 P.M. with Diesel.
November 6 thru January 3, 1988, Week-ends & Holidays, 2:00 to 9:00 P.M., Week-days 4:00 to 9:00 P.M. Closed Thanksgiving & Christmas, open New Years Day.
Railfan Week-end and Railroad Flea Market held June 20-21, 1987.

Fare: Admission to grounds, train ride and museum: Adults $7.50, Children $5.00.

Locomotives: #3, 0-4-4T, Vulcan (1913), ex-Monson. #4, 0-4-0T, Vulcan (1918), ex-Monson. #7, 2-4-4T, Baldwin (1913), ex-Bridgton & Harrison. #8, 2-4-4T, Baldwin (1924), ex-Bridgton & Harrison.

Train: Wooden open platform combine, coaches, open cars, caboose.

Displays: The Edaville complex contains an excellent indoor railroad museum, an extensive fire museum and a collection of antique automobiles. Standard gauge railroad equipment on display includes Boston & Maine streamliner "Flying Yankee" and B.&M. 2-6-0, #1455, Alco (1907).
Kenton T. Harrison, Curator

✔Refreshments
✔Gift Shop
✔Picnic Area
✔Restaurant

Edaville Railroad
Box 7
South Carver, MA 02366
Phone (617) 866-4526

Location: The Providence & Worcester Railroad Co., first chartered in 1844, is now a common-carrier freight railroad operating in the States of Massachusetts, Rhode Island and Connecticut.

Ride: A number of passenger excursions are offered over the railroad using reconditioned modern cross-country coaches, a dining car and a round-end observation car. Trips vary from all-day journeys to specific destinations, to shorter 3-hour round trips.

Schedule: All trips depart from the P.&W. railyards located at 382 Southbridge St., Worcester, MA. Train runs to U.S.S. Nautilus Submarine Base in Groton, CT on September 26. Fall Foliage Trains run on October 4, 10, 11, 17 & 18, leave at 11:30 A.M. and 2:30 P.M. Routes include Worcester to Gardner, MA, Plainfield, CT or Woonsocket, RI, depending upon the brilliance of the color. Santa Claus Special operates December 19. Train is also available for Special Charters.

Fare: Varies with trip. Write for timetable containing schedule and fares for all 1987 trips.

Locomotives: Modern diesel power including EMD GP-38, GP-38-2s, GP-9s, G.E. U18-B, G.E. B23-7 and MLW M420-Rs.

Train: Former Amtrak cross-country coaches, dining car and souvenir cars, ex-Northern Pacific round-end observation car.

Note: Tickets may be ordered by mail in advance. Consult 1987 P.&W. timetables.

✔Refreshments
✔Gift Shop on train
✔Dining Car

Providence & Worcester R.R.
P.O. Box 1188
Worcester, MA 01601
Phone (617) 755-4000

 Worcester

87

MICHIGAN, CLINTON
Southern Michigan Railroad

Diesel, scheduled
Standard gauge

Location: Clinton is located in the southern part of the state, on U.S. 12, about 20 miles southwest of Ann Arbor.

Ride: A 10-mile, 2-hour round trip between Clinton and Tecumseh over a former New York Central branchline. The railroad runs adjacent to the River Raisin, crosses a 116-ft. trestle over the scenic Ford millpond and wildlife area. Line then crosses the Evans Creek bridge into the historic town of Tecumseh. Passengers may make a stopover at either end of the line. A longer trip is offered Saturday nights over the line south of Tecumseh, crossing the River Raisin on a 300 ft. long steel bridge.

Schedule: Saturdays, Sundays & Holidays, May 2 to September 27. Southbound trips depart Clinton every 45 minutes, Noon to 3:45 P.M. Northbound trains leave Tecumseh every 45 minutes, 12:45 to 4:30 P.M. Trips south of Tecumseh leave Saturdays at 6:00 P.M.

Fare: Adults $4.00, Students (5-18) $2.00. Tecumseh south, Adults $6.00, Students $3.00. Group rates, charters and season passes available.

Locomotives: #8201, 8203, RS-2 diesels, Alco (1950), ex-A.A., G.B.&W. #57, 35-ton diesel, Plymouth (1938), ex-Hayes-Albion Corp.

Train: Delaware, Lackawanna & Western coaches #4345, 4365 (1920). New Haven caboose, New York Central caboose. Maintenance-of-way gang cars are also used.

Displays: #20, 21, RS-1 diesels, Alco (1950), ex-Ann Arbor. Restored railway motor cars from various railroads. Museum with numerous railroad artifacts and memorabilia. Museum hours, Daily 9:30 A.M. to 5:30 P.M., Sundays, Noon to 5:30 P.M.

✔Refreshments
✔Gift Shop
✔Picnic Area
✔Memberships

Southern Michigan Railroad Society
P.O. Box 434
Clinton, MI 49236
Phone (517) 456-7029

 Ann Arbor

88

MICHIGAN, DEARBORN
Greenfield Village R.R.
Henry Ford Museum

Steam, scheduled
Museum, Railway Exhibits
Standard gauge

Courtesy of the Henry Ford Museum

Location: The Museum is ½-mile south of U.S. 12 (Michigan Ave.) between Southfield Road and Oakwood Blvd. in Dearborn.

Ride: A 2½-mile, 20-minute ride around the grounds of the world-famous Greenfield Village.

Schedule: Museum and Village: Daily, year-round, 9:00 A.M. to 5:00 P.M. Closed U.S. Thanksgiving, Christmas, New Year's Day. Steam train operates Daily, April through October.

Admission: Museum: Adults $8.50, Children (5-12) $4.50, Seniors $7.00, under 5 free. Village: Same as above. Memberships and 2-day rates available.

Fare: Steam train: Adults $1.50, Children $1.00.

Locomotives: #1, 4-4-0, built c. 1876, rebuilt Ford Motor Co. 1920's.
#3, 0-6-4T, Mason-Fairlie (1873), Calumet & Hecla Mining.
#8, 0-6-0, Baldwin (1914), ex-Detroit & Mackinac R.R.

Train: Specially constructed open excursion type cars and two c. 1890 wooden coaches.

Displays: The world-famous Henry Ford Museum is a general museum of American history occupying about 12 acres under one roof. Greenfield Village is a 230 acre outdoor museum comprised of over 80 historic structures. There are a number of steam locomotives exhibited in the Museum along with numerous motor vehicles. The largest locomotive in the Museum is #1601, a 2-6-6-6 Allegheny type built by Lima in 1941 for the Chesapeake & Ohio R.R.

Randy Mason, Curator, Transportation Collection

✔Refreshments
✔Gift Shop
✔Restaurants
✔Memberships

Henry Ford Museum & Greenfield Village
P.O. Box 1970
Dearborn, MI 48121
Phone (313) 271-1620

 Dearborn

Photo by Taro Yamasaki

Location: Trolleys operate on Washington Boulevard and Jefferson Avenue in downtown Detroit. The line is operated by the Detroit Dept. of Transportation and all motormen are also qualified bus drivers.

Ride: A 1-mile, 12 minute ride in each direction between the Renaissance Center, Cobo Hall and Grand Circus Park. The line is single track, primarily curbside and in median, with a passing siding at Cobo Hall and at the Book Cadillac Hotel along the route.

Schedule: Cars operate Daily, 7:30 A.M. to 6:00 P.M. on week-days and 10:00 A.M. to 6:00 P.M. on week-ends. Cars run at 10-minute intervals. Special service run for conventions and cars may also be chartered.

Fare: Exact fare, 45¢ each direction. No bus transfers issued or accepted. No multi-ride pass issued. Senior Citizens (over 65) and "babes in arms" ride free of charge.

Trolleys: Trolleys are single-truck cars which formerly ran in Lisbon, Portugal. Car #247 is an open car and runs in late Spring and Summer, weather permitting. Car #14 is a 1904 double-deck tram which came from the Burton & Ashby Light Railway in England. Additional cars are on hand for expanded service and/or for spare parts. The Lisbon cars were built in the U.S. by J.G. Brill Co. or St. Louis Car Co. between 1899 and 1927.

Displays: Non-operating cars can be viewed through glass walls of the carbarn at the north end of the line. A free brochure titled "The Trolley Returns to Downtown Detroit" is available upon request from the motorman, as well as a hand-out describing the double-deck tram from England.

Claryce Ossman, Superintendent Scheduling, Planning & Marketing.

Detroit Dept. of Transportation
1301 E. Warren
Detroit, MI 48207
Phone (313) 935-4567

 Detroit

MICHIGAN, FLINT
Huckleberry Railroad

Steam, scheduled
36" gauge

Photo by Loring M. Lawrence

Location: The train runs through the scenic Genesee Recreation Area northeast of Flint. From I-475 take Exit 11 (Carpenter Road). Go east 1 mile to Bray Road, then north ½ mile to entrance.

Ride: A ¾-hour, 10-mile round trip departing from the depot at Crossroads Village. The train runs over a section of Pere Marquette R.R. roadbed constructed in the mid-1800's.

Schedule: Daily, May 20 thru September 7. Train departs hourly, 11:00 A.M. to 4:00 P.M. on week-days, Noon to 5:00 P.M. on week-ends & holidays. Annual Railfan Days, August 15-16, 1987. Re-opens for "Christmas at Crossroads" on November 27-29, December 4-6, 11-13, 18-20, 26-27.

Fare: Adults $5.95, Seniors $4.95, Children $3.95. Ticket includes Village admission and train ride.

Locomotives: #2, 4-6-0, Baldwin (1920), ex-Alaska R.R. #152.
#4, 2-8-0, Baldwin (1904), ex-Potosi & Rio Verde (Mexico).
#464, 2-8-2, Baldwin (1903), ex-Denver & Rio Grande Western.
#3, 2-6-0, Brooks (1894), ex-Quincy & Torch Lake.

Train: Restored open and closed platform vintage coaches from Denver & Rio Grande Western, Rio Grande Southern and several Mexican narrow-gauge railroads.

Displays: Crossroads Village is a re-creation of a typical Genesee County community from 1860-1880. The Village includes 24 authentic buildings populated with the villagers in period costumes going about their every day activities.

Kenneth J. Smithee, Director

✔Refreshments
✔Gift Shop
✔Picnic Area
✔Restaurant
✔Camp Grounds

TRAIN

Genesee County Parks & Recreation Comm.
G-5055 Branch Road
Flint, MI 48506
Phone (313) 736-1700

MICHIGAN, MT. CLEMENS
Michigan Transit Museum

Electric, Diesel, scheduled
Standard gauge

Photo by William J. Zombory

Location: Train departs from the Caboose Depot, ¾-mile north of Mt. Clemens on North Gratiot Ave. Use North River Road exit of I-94.

Ride: Unique trolley-train ride provides an 8-mile, 45-minute trip through farmlands, a park and runs near Selfridge Air National Guard Base. Eastbound, train is controlled from "El" cars, with the diesel locomotive providing the electricity. Westbound, locomotive powers train in normal fashion. Also located along the route is the Selfridge Military Air Museum.

Schedule: Sunday afternoons only, May 24 through September 27. Train leaves on the hour from 1:00 to 4:00 P.M.

Fare: Adults $3.00, Children (4-12) $1.75, under 4 free. Charter rates on request.

Locomotives: #1807, S-1 diesel, Alco (1941), ex-Alco plant switcher.

Trolleys: #761, ex-Chicago, North Shore & Milwaukee car (1929). #262, ex-Detroit P.C.C. car. #761 and #262 are not presently on display.

Train: Train consists of 2 former Chicago "El" cars, #4442 and #4450. The diesel locomotive provides the power for the electric cars one-way, then propels train for the remainder of the trip.

Displays: The group has leased the Mt. Clemens Edison Depot, built in 1859.The depot, containing artifacts of area railroading, is open Sundays from 2:00 to 4:00 P.M. Grand Trunk Western caboose #77058 (1900) is used as a ticket office.

✔Gift Shop
✔Memberships

Michigan Transit Museum, Inc.
P.O. Box 12
Fraser, MI 48026
Phone (313) 463-1863
(313) 466-5035

Photo by Ray Plamondon

Location: The City of Traverse City is located on the shores of Grand Traverse Bay in northwestern Michigan. Clinch Park is a unique waterfront park maintained by the City. It features a native wildlife zoo, swimming beach, yacht harbor, boat ramp, museum and a miniature train ride "The Spirit of Traverse City".

Ride: A 15" gauge steam train provides a one-half-mile ride around Clinch Park Zoo.

Schedule: Train operates Daily, Memorial Day through Labor Day (weather permitting) from 10:00 A.M. to 6:00 P.M.

Fare: Adults 75¢, Children 50¢, under 3 free.

Locomotives: #400, 4-4-2, built by Dan Russell Boiler Works, Boston, Mass. in 1949. This steam locomotive is oil-fired.

Train: Three passenger cars, each holding 12 passengers.

Displays: The Con Foster Museum offers exhibits and programs on the history of the local area. Exhibits include prehistoric artifacts, the logging and lumbering era, early settlement, shipping and other displays.

✔Refreshments
✔Picnic Area

City of Traverse City
400 Boardman
Traverse City, MI 49685
Phone (616) 922-4905

Photo by Loring M. Lawrence

Location: The Museum is located at 506 W. Michigan St., next to the former Duluth Union Depot, now the St. Louis County Heritage & Arts Center.

Displays: The Museum features a number of interesting and historic locomotives and cars, under cover, permitting viewing year-round. Located here is the Great Northern's famous "William Crooks" locomotive and cars of 1861 as well as the Northern Pacific's first engine, the "Minnetonka". Huge Duluth, Missabe & Iron Range #227, a 2-8-8-4, is displayed with revolving drive wheels and recorded sound. The Milwaukee Road's first mainline electric locomotive, #10200 is here on display. Other exhibits include an 1887 steam rotary snowplow, other steam, diesel and electric engines, plus a Railway Post Office car, a dining car, freight cars, work equipment and much railroadiana. There is also an operating electric single-truck streetcar.

Schedule: Museum is open Daily, year-round. Monday through Saturday, 10:00 A.M. to 5:00 P.M. Sundays, 1:00 to 5:00 P.M. except June through September, 10:00 A.M. to 5:00 P.M.

Admission: Adults $3.50, Senior Citizens $2.75, Children (6-17) $1.75, under 5 free, Family $10.00. Admission price includes adjacent Heritage and Arts Center.

Thomas Gannon, Curator

✔Gift Shop
✔Memberships

TRAIN

Lake Superior Museum of Transportation
506 W. Michigan St.
Duluth, MN 55812
Phone (218) 727-8025
or (218) 727-0687

MINNESOTA, DULUTH
Lake Superior & Mississippi R.R.

Diesel, scheduled
Standard gauge

Photo by Dave Schauer

Location: Trains depart from a site 6 miles southwest of downtown Duluth on Grand Ave., Route 23, right across from the Lake Superior Zoological Gardens. Park in the Western Waterfront Trail parking lot.

Ride: A 12-mile, 1½-hour round trip which follows the scenic St. Louis River to New Duluth. The line was first built in 1870 as the Lake Superior & Mississippi R.R., later part of the Northern Pacific and Burlington Northern.

Schedule: Saturdays & Sundays during July, August and September. Trains depart at 11:30 A.M., 2:00 & 4:00 P.M.

Fare: Adults $4.00, Seniors $3.50, Children $2.00.
Charter rates available.

Locomotives: #46, 45-ton diesel, General Electric (1946).
#935, SW-9 diesel, E.M.D. (1952), ex-Minn-Tac Mining.

Train: Heavyweight coaches from D.M.&I.R. and C.N., S.P.&S. baggage car, open-air gondola and Northern Pacific caboose.

Displays: See Lake Superior Transportation Museum.

🖊Refreshments
🖊Gift Shop
🖊Memberships

Lake Superior & Mississippi R.R.
506 West Michigan St.
Duluth, MN 55812
Phone (218) 727-8025

Location: Como-Harriet Streetcar Line leaves from 42nd & Queen Ave. South at Lake Harriet in South Minneapolis.

Ride: A 2-mile round trip on a restored portion of the old Twin City Rapid Transit Co.'s historic Como-Harriet line. The 15-minute ride is over a private right of way through a scenic wooded area between Lakes Calhoun and Harriet.

Schedule: Memorial Day week-end thru Labor Day week-end; Saturdays, 3:30 P.M. to dusk; Sundays & Holidays, 12:30 P.M. to dusk; Monday thru Friday, 6:30 P.M. to dusk. Week-ends only in September & October.

Fare: Adults, Children 50¢, in arms free.

Trolleys: #1300, Twin City Rapid Transit (1908). #265, Duluth Street Railway (1915). Both built by TCRT Snelling Shops.

Displays: Minnehaha Depot, built in 1875 by Milwaukee Road. Located near Minnehaha Falls, the depot is manned by Museum members Sunday afternoons, Memorial Day to Labor Day.

Other: Museum owns much additional rolling stock, including streetcars, locomotives, passenger and freight cars and busses.

✔Refreshments adjacent
✔Picnic Area adjacent
✔Memberships

Minnesota Transportation Museum
P.O. Box 1796
St. Paul, MN 55101

 Minneapolis

MINNESOTA, STILLWATER
Minnesota Transportation Museum

Location: Stillwater is located on the Minnesota-Wisconsin border and is about 15 miles east of Minneapolis. Trains load from North Main St. in downtown Stillwater.

Ride: A one hour to one and one-half hour train ride, powered by a steam locomotive, a vintage diesel or a "doodlebug".

Schedule: Saturdays, Sundays & Holidays, Memorial Day through September.

Fare: Adults $6.00 or less, depending on length of ride and equipment used. Children, Seniors and Family discounts. Show your membership card in any of the museums listed in the "Steam Directory" and receive an additional 50¢ discount.

Locomotives: #328, 4-6-0, Alco (1907), ex-Northern Pacific Ry.
#9735, gas-electric car, ex-Burlington Route.

Train: M.T.M. steel coaches.

Displays: Jackson Street Roundhouse — this is the grand opening year for public display of a working railroad roundhouse. The building is located at Jackson St. & Pennsylvania Ave. in St. Paul. Take the Pennsylvania Ave. exit from I-35E, then go one block west.

Minnesota Transportation Museum
P.O. Box 1796
St. Paul, MN 55101

Location: Ash Grove is located on U.S. 160, 15 miles west of Springfield in the Ozark Mountains of southern Missouri. The Museum is located at 500 Walker St. in Ash Grove, on the Springfield-Kansas City main-line of the former St. Louis-San Francisco Ry. (Frisco Lines), now Burlington Northern.

Displays: The Museum is the only such facility devoted exclusively to memorabilia of the Frisco Lines. Housed in a building reminiscent of many small town depots, the Museum has on display over 1000 items of Frisco and Frisco-related memorabilia. There is a dining car display, a mock-up of an open Pullman section and a ticket agent's window and telegrapher's bay.

Schedule: June 1 to August 31: Open Daily except Monday & Tuesday from *10:00 A.M. to 5:00 P.M. September 1 to May 31: Open Saturdays & Sundays only, *10:00 A.M. to 5:00 P.M. (*Opens 2:00 P.M. on Sunday).

Admission: No charge. Donations appreciated.

Note: The Frisco Railroad Museum, Inc. is not affiliated with the St. Louis-San Francisco Railway Co., the Burlington Northern Railroad Co., or any of its subsidiaries.

✔Refreshments
✔Picnic Area
✔Memberships

Frisco Railroad Museum
P.O. Box 276
Ash Grove, MO 65604
Phone (417) 672-3110

Photo by David J. Neubauer

Location: Glencoe (St. Louis County) is located about 25 miles west of St. Louis via I-44. At Eureka exit, take Route 109 north 3½-miles to Old State Road, make 2 right turns to the depot on Washington St.-Grand Ave.

Ride: A 2.8 mile, 30-minute round trip over a former Missouri Pacific right-of-way. The mini-steam trains run along the scenic Meramac River. The locomotive is turned on a turntable at each end of the line.

Schedule: Sundays only, May through October. Six scheduled trains operate from 1:00 to 4:20 P.M.

Fare: Adults, Children $1.50, under 3 free.
Cloth patch (logo) available for $1.75.

Locomotives: #171, 4-4-0, (coal), Elgin, IL (1907);
#180, 4-4-0, (coal), (1922);
#300, 4-4-2, (oil), Alton, IL (1958);
#400, 4-6-2, (oil), Shalford, U.K. (1925);
#802, SW-8, (gasoline), Wood River, IL (1982);
#82, 0-4-0, (gasoline), Wood River, IL (1981);
#X-41, 0-4-0, (gasoline), Berkeley, MO (1945).

Train: Passenger coaches and wooden-benched flat cars.

Displays: Despite its small size, this railroad is authentically operated and maintained. Standard crossing signals protect a street crossing in downtown Glencoe. Radio frequency is 151.955.

David J. Neubauer, V.P. - Operations

Mailing Address:
✔Memberships
Wabash Frisco & Pacific Ry.
c/o David J. Neubauer
1569 Ville Angela Lane
✔Large SASE for photo brochure
Hazelwood, MO 63042
and information sheet
Phone (314) 587-3538 (Operating Sundays)

MISSOURI, JACKSON
St. Louis Iron Mountain & Southern Ry.

Steam, scheduled
Standard gauge

Location: Jackson is located in southeast Missouri, a few miles from Cape Girardeau on Routes 61, 25 and 72. The site is just west of Interstate 55.

Ride: Steam powered passenger train runs from Jackson on three differing length runs over a former Missouri Pacific branchline. Train makes a 10-mile, 1¼-hour run from Jackson to Gordonville, a 20-mile, 2-hour round trip to Dutchtown and a 28-mile, 3-hour round trip to Delta.

Schedule: Saturdays, Sundays & Holidays, April to October.
Train leaves Jackson Saturdays at 10:00 A.M. for Gordonville, 3:00 P.M. for Delta.
Leaves Jackson Sundays & Holidays at 1:00 & 2:30 for Gordonville, 4:00 P.M. for Dutchtown.

Fare: Varies with trip. Adults $7.00, $10.00, $15.00. Children (3-10) $3.00, $4.00, $7.00. One-way fares also available.

Locomotives: #5, 2-4-2, Porter (1946), ex-Central Illinois Public Service, ex-Crab Orchard & Egyptian R.R.

Train: Two former Illinois Central steel coaches, ex-Missouri Pacific caboose.

✔Refreshments
✔Gift Shop
✔Picnic Area

St. Louis Iron Mountain & Southern Ry.
P.O. Box 244
Jackson, MO 63755
Phone (314) 243-1688

Location: On I-270 **from** the north, use Big Bend Road Exit, turn right to Barrett Station Road. On I-270 **from** the south, use Dougherty Ferry Road Exit, turn left to Barrett Station Road.

Displays: The National Museum of Transport is owned by St. Louis County and many improvements have been made in the site. On static display at the Museum is an extensive and important collection of all forms of transportation equipment. There are over 70 steam locomotives from ancient 4-4-0's to some of the largest and newest steam and diesel engines in the country. In addition to locomotives, there are passenger and freight cars, motor trucks, aircraft, streetcars, buses and fire apparatus. Frisco Lines #1522, shown above left is currently being restored to operating condition. This is one of the country's largest transportation museums.

Schedule: Open Daily, year-round, 9:00 A.M. to 5:00 P.M. Closed Thanksgiving, Christmas and New Year's Day.

Admission: Age 13 through 64 $2.00. Age 65 and over $1.00. Age 5 through 12 $1.00.

Locomotives: There are engines here of every description. The "Daniel Nason", a 4-4-0, was built in 1858. D.L.&W. #952, a 4-4-0 camelback, built in 1905 was displayed at the 1939 N.Y. World's Fair. There is a Burlington Zephyr train as well as Southern Ry. "F" unit diesel No. 6100. One of the Santa Fe's largest steam engines, 2-10-4 No. 5011 is here. Latest engine to be received is huge Union Pacific "Centennial" diesel No. 6944. This largest diesel ever built joins U.P. "Big Boy" No. 4006, largest steam engine built.

Note: A locomotive and several cars are now on display at the restored St. Louis Union Station.

Capt. William S. Streckfus, Director

✔Refreshments
✔Gift Shop
✔Memberships in Transport
  Museum Assn.

National Museum of Transport
3015 Barrett Station Road
St. Louis, MO 63122
Phone (314) 965-7998

 St. Louis

Location: Train leaves from the Briscoe Station, on Riverview Blvd. 1½ miles south of I-270 bridge over the Mississippi River.

Ride: A 6-mile, 1-hour round trip on the tracks of the St. Louis Water Works Railway. The Southern Division connects with the B.N. in North St. Louis and a view of the distant downtown skyline with the Gateway Arch is possible. The Northern Division runs along the bank of the Mississippi River and affords the passengers a view of Dam #27, the largest rock fill dam in the United States.

Schedule: Train operates on the second Sunday of the month, April through October, from 1:00 to 5:00 P.M. A special "Hayride on a Train" is held on the second Sunday of November as a fund raising event. It is underwritten by the American Association of Railroaders, Inc.

Fare: Donation.

Locomotives: 45-ton General Electric diesel, ex-U.S. Navy.
80-ton Whitcomb, ex-Missouri Portland Cement.
EMD F-7A Diesels #406 & #410, ex-Chicago & North Western Ry.

Train: C.N.J. open-window coach, Cotton Belt flatcar with bench seating, Cotton belt gondola, N.&W. caboose and Frisco transfer caboose.

Stored Equipment: Porter 0-4-0 fireless locomotive #3, P.R.R. lounge-sleeper, B.&O. caboose, Frisco transfer cabooses, 35-ton Plymouth gas-mechanical engine, ex-U.S. Navy and various motor cars.

Note: A landing site and boat launching ramp adjacent to Briscoe Station provides an opportunity for Mississippi River access.

Richard A. Eichhorst, General Manager

✔Gift Shop
✔Picnic Area
✔Memberships

Amtrak━━ St. Louis

Mailing Address:
St. Louis & Chain of Rocks R.R.
3422 Osage Street
St. Louis, MO 63118
Phone (314) 752-3148

Location: Train leaves from depot at 301 E. First St. in Fremont, about 35 miles west of Omaha.

Ride: A 30-mile, 4-hour round trip from Fremont to the historic town of Hooper. Train crosses the Mormon Trail and runs through the beautiful Elkhorn River valley. This line was formerly a branch of the Chicago & North Western Ry.

Schedule: Saturdays, Sundays & Holidays, April 18 thru October 25. From April 18 thru May 17 (diesel) and September 12 thru October 25 (steam), train leaves Fremont Saturdays 11:00 A.M., Sundays 2:00 P.M.
From May 23 thru September 7, steam train leaves Fremont Saturdays and Holidays 11:00 A.M. & 5:00 P.M., Sundays 2:00 P.M. Week-days (except Monday), diesel train makes shorter trip to Nickerson at 2:00 P.M.

Fare: To Hooper: Adults $10.00, Children $5.00, under 3 free.
To Nickerson: Adults $6.00, Children $4.00, under 3 free.

Locomotives: #1702, 2-8-0, Baldwin (1942), ex-U.S. Army, ex-Reader R.R.
#302, GP-9 diesel, EMD (1959), ex-Milwaukee Road.
#2121, SW1200 diesel, EMD (1959), ex-Soo Line.
#88C, F-7 diesel, EMD (1949), ex-Milwaukee Road (under restoration).

Train: Lackawanna commuter coaches, 1920's C.&N.W. heavyweight coaches, 1940's Milwaukee Road lightweight coaches, steel and wooden cabooses.

Other: Path Finder Dinner Train operates Friday and Saturday nights. Train consists of elegantly appointed dining and lounge cars. Reservations required.
The Fremont & Elkhorn Valley is Nebraska's longest and largest steam excursion railroad.

✔Refreshments
✔Gift Shop
✔Picnic Area
✔Camping Nearby

Fremont & Elkhorn Valley R.R.
P.O. Box 939
Fremont, NE 68025
Phone (402) 727-0615

NEBRASKA, GRAND ISLAND
Nebraska Midland R.R.

Steam, scheduled
36" gauge

Photo by Thomas R. Schultz

Location: The Nebraska Midland R.R. operates on the grounds of the Stuhr Museum of the Prairie Pioneer. The Museum is located 4 miles north of I-80 at the junction of U.S. Routes 281 and 34 at Grand Island, Nebraska.

Ride: A 4-mile, 30-minute ride across 200 acres of prairieland. The train departs from the 1887 Kearney & Black Hills depot of the Museum's reconstructed Railroad Town.

Schedule: Train operates Daily, May 1 through September 30. Several runs are made each day between 11:00 A.M. and 4:30 P.M.

Fare: Adults $2.00, Students (7-16) $1.00, under 7 free. Train fares are in addition to the General Admission to the grounds, Adults $5.00, Students (7-16) $2.50, under 7 free.

Locomotives: #69, 2-8-0, Baldwin (1908), ex-White Pass & Yukon.

Train: 1897 coach (ex-F.&C.C. #65), 1874 baggage car (ex-C.&S.), 3 open excursion cars (ex-D.&R.G.W. gondolas).

Displays: Standard gauge railroad equipment includes #437, 2-8-0, Baldwin (1902), Union Pacific R.R.; 1872 St. Joseph-Grand Island boarding car; 1912 Union Pacific caboose. Also Union Pacific passenger equipment including the Pullman Car "Lake Crystal".

Note: The Stuhr Museum also features Indian and old west exhibits, antique auto and farm machinery collection and over 60 acres of indoor and outdoor exhibits which interpret pioneer life in Nebraska.

Jack A. Learned, Executive Director

✔Refreshments
✔Gift Shop
✔Picnic Area

Nebraska Midland R.R.
Stuhr Museum of the Prairie Pioneer
3133 West Highway 34
Grand Island, NE 68801
Phone (308) 381-5316

Photo courtesy Union Pacific System

Location: The Union Pacific Historical Museum is located on the first floor of Union Pacific System's 12-story headquarters building at 1416 Dodge Street, in downtown Omaha.

Displays: The recently renovated Museum tells the story of the Union Pacific Railroad and the role it played in building the West from the days of Abraham Lincoln and General Grenville Dodge to the present. The Museum features a model of Lincoln's funeral car, a stuffed buffalo, General Dodge's surveying instruments, a large working model railroad, a railroad auditor's office from the 1880's, historic Union Pacific model trains, cars and locomotives. Also a model of a Centralized Traffic Control board and other artifacts and photos showing the growth and operations of the Union Pacific.

Admission: No charge.

Schedule: Open year-round Monday through Friday from 9:00 A.M. to 5:00 P.M. and Saturdays from 9:00 A.M. to 1:00 P.M. Closed Sundays and Holidays. Group tours may be scheduled in advance.

Union Pacific Historical Museum
1416 Dodge Street
Omaha, NE 68179
Phone (402) 271-3530

 Omaha

Museum photo by Daun Bohall

Location: The Museum is located on South Carson St. (U.S. 395) at Fairview Drive, opposite the Silver City Mall.

Displays: The Museum contains 22 pieces of original Virginia & Truckee R.R. rolling stock, of which 12, situated on 4 tracks, are visible to the public. Most of this historic collection of locomotives and cars were once owned by Hollywood motion picture studios. Restoration of the equipment is well underway. The museum also houses an exhibit area featuring photos, artifacts and memorabilia of the famous V.&T.R.R.

Locomotives: V&T #25, 4-6-0, Baldwin (1905). Restored, operating.
V&T #18, "Dayton", 4-4-0, Central Pacific (1873). Restored.
V&T #22, "Inyo", 4-4-0, Baldwin (1875). Restored, operating.
C&TL&F Co. #2, "Glenbrook", 2-6-0, Baldwin (1875), narrow-gauge.

Rolling Stock: V&T coaches #4, 11, 12, 18; Express #14; Caboose-coach #9; Mail-baggage #21; Caboose #24; Motor car #99 and 9 freight cars. Also a French "40 & 8" boxcar, LV&T coach #30, N-C-O coach #52, C&C boxcar #303, SP ng boxcars #4 & 426, SP ng stock cars #159 & 162, C&C baggage-mail-express #3 and motor car "Washoe Zephyr".

Schedule: Open Fridays, Saturdays, Sundays & Holidays, May 22 through November 1 from 8:30 A.M. to 4:30 P.M.

Fare: Steam train: Adults $2.50, Children (6-11) $1.00, under 6 free.
Motor car: Adults $1.00, Children (6-11) 50¢, under 6 free.

Operation: Motor car #50 operates every week-end during the season. Restored V&T steam engines #22 and/or #25 operate May 23-24, July 3-5, August 1-2 & 15-16, September 5-6, October 3-4 & October 30-November 1.

Richard C. Datin, Curator

✔Gift Shop
✔Trailer Parking

Nevada State Railroad Museum
Capitol Complex
Carson City, NV 89710
Phone (702) 885-4810 or 885-5168

Location: Ely is located in eastern Nevada on U.S. 93. Trains leave from the foot of 11th St. East and Avenue A in East Ely.
The Nevada Northern Ry. operated a 150-mile line which ran both north and south from Ely. Portions of this line have now been re-opened for passenger excursions.

Ride: Steam trains will operate over two routes this season. An 18-mile round trip from Ely to Copper Flat via Robinson Canyon and Ruth, through mountainous terrain. Also, a 27-mile, 2-hour round trip to McGill Jct. and over a branchline to the smelter town of McGill.

Schedule: Trains will operate on May 23-25, July 4-5, August 1-2, September 5-7 & 26-27, 1987. Five departures on each day.
To Copper Flat: 9:00 A.M. & 2:00 P.M.
To McGill: 11:00 A.M. & 4:00 P.M.
"Twilight Limited" leaves 6:00 P.M. for Copper Flat and McGill Jct.

Fare: To Copper Flat: Adults $12.00, Children $4.00, under 5 free.
To McGill: Adults $14.00, Children $4.00, under 5 free.

Locomotives: #40, 4-6-0, Baldwin (1910), Nevada Northern Ry.
Steam locomotive and train have been in inside storage for 46 years.
#105, Alco RS-2 diesel; #109, Alco RS-3; #802, Baldwin S-12 diesel.
Stand-by diesels from Kennecott Copper Co.

Train: Wooden baggage/RPO car, wooden coach, steel lounge/snack-bar car, open car with benches.

Displays: Steam, diesel and electric locomotives, 1907 steam rotary snow-plow, 1910 Jordan spreader. Over 60 pieces of antique passenger, freight and work equipment. General offices, depot, machine shops and round-house. Museum provides guided walk-thru tours every day from May 18 to October 4, 1987.

Note: The former Nevada Northern Ry. and Kennecott Copper Co. facilities are now owned by the non-profit White Pine Historical Railroad Foundation, Inc.

✔Refreshments
✔Gift Shop
✔Memberships

Nevada Northern Railway Museum
P.O. Box 40
East Ely, NV 89315
Phone (702) 289-2085

NEVADA, VIRGINIA CITY
Virginia & Truckee Railroad Co.

Steam, scheduled
Standard gauge

Location: The depot is located at Washington and "F" Sts. in the historic mining town of Virginia City.

Ride: A 3½-mile, 30-minute round trip over a portion of the legendary Virginia & Truckee Railroad. The train travels through the heart of the historic Comstock mining area of Nevada over the 118-year-old roadbed of the old V.&T. Trip has now been extended through Tunnel #4. A knowledgeable Conductor gives a running commentary on the line and answers questions relating to the mining history of the area.

Schedule: Daily, May 23 through September 30. Week-ends during October. Train makes 10 to 11 runs each day from 10:30 A.M. to 6:00 P.M.

Fare: Adults $2.75, Children $1.50, under 5 free. All-day pass $6.00.

Locomotives: #29, 2-8-0, Baldwin (1916), ex-Longview, Portland & Northern.
#30, 0-6-0 (1919), ex-Southern Pacific.

Train: One open car and two semi-closed cars.

Displays: Northwestern Pacific combine and coach, vintage 1888. Ex-Tonopah & Tidewater coach, ex-Northern Pacific caboose.

🖊Refreshments
🖊Gift Shop
🖊Picnic Area
🖊Trailer Parking

TRA🖊N

Virginia & Truckee Railroad Co., Inc.
P.O. Box 467
Virginia City, NV 89440
Phone (702) 847-0380

Location: Located on Route 3, one mile north of North Woodstock, N.H. in the heart of the scenic White Mountains.

Ride: A 2-mile, 30-minute ride leaving from a beautiful depot at Clark's Trading Post. Train crosses a 120 ft. covered bridge and climbs a 2% grade into the woods.

Schedule: Steam train operates Daily, July 1 to Labor Day, also week-ends September through mid-October. Trains run every hour. 1930 Reo railbus operates week-ends May, June, week-days September as needed.

Admission: Adults $5.00, Children (6-11) $4.00, under 6 free.

Locomotives: #4, 2-truck Heisler (1927), ex-International Shoe Co. #6, Climax, ex-Beebe River R.R. #3, ex-East Branch & Lincoln.

Train: Open excursion cars.

Displays: Clark's Trading Post features trained bears, a fire museum, an Americana museum, a haunted house, an antique photo parlor, a candy shop-ice cream parlor and much more. Railway rolling stock display includes caboose, box cars and flat cars, all of wooden construction, also disconnected trucks for hauling logs. Also on the site is a 1920's era garage and an illusion building called Merlin's Mansion.

W. Murray Clark, Vice-President & Treasurer

✔Refreshments
✔Gift Shop
✔Picnic Area

White Mountain Central R.R.
Box 1
North Woodstock, NH 03262
Phone (603) 745-2201

NEW HAMPSHIRE, MEREDITH
Winnipesaukee Railroad

**Diesel, scheduled
Standard gauge**

Location: Trains leave from Meredith and Weirs Beach on U.S. Route 3. From Interstate 93, use Exits 20 or 23.

Ride: Winnipesaukee Railroad passenger trains operate along the shores of Lake Winnipesaukee in central New Hampshire. During the Summer, trains operate an 18-mile, 1¾-hour round trip between Meredith and Lakeport.
During the Fall season, train ride runs from Weirs Beach north to Plymouth, a 36-mile, 3-hour round trip.

Schedule: Saturdays, Sundays & Holidays, May 23-June 14 and September 12-20. Daily operation, June 27 through September 7. Departs Meredith 9:30, 11:30 A.M., 1:30, 3:30 P.M. Departs Weirs Beach hourly, 10:00 A.M. to 4:00 P.M.
Evening train runs Tuesday, Wednesday & Thursday, June 27-September 3 from Meredith at 7:00 P.M.
Fall schedule: Daily, September 26-October 18. Lv. Weirs Beach 1:00 P.M., lv. Meredith 1:15 P.M. Additional train, Week-ends and Holidays, lv. Weirs Beach 10:00 A.M., Meredith 10:15 A.M.

Fare: Regular Train: Adults $6.00, Children (5-12) $4.00, under 5 free.
Fall Foliage: Adults $11.00, Children (5-12) $8.00, under 5 free.
Write to railroad for complete schedule of trains and fares.

Locomotives: #557, RS-3 diesel, Alco (1952), ex-Maine Central.
#2, 44-ton diesel, G.E. (1943), ex-U.S. Govt.
#1008, S-1 diesel, Alco (1949), ex-Portland Terminal.

Train: Former Jersey Central, New York Central and Lackawanna open-window day coaches.

Displays: 1893 Boston & Maine baggage car, Boston & Maine milk car, cabooses from Bangor & Aroostook, Lehigh & New England and Rutland Railroad.

✔Gift Shop
✔Picnic Area

Winnipesaukee Railroad
P.O. Box 6268
Lakeport, NH 03246
Phone (603) 528-2330

Photo by John E. Helbok

Location: The Cog Railway leaves from Base Station off U.S. Route 302 east of Twin Mountain, N.H.

Ride: The world's first mountain climbing railway, completed in 1869 is still 100% steam powered. The train ascends New England's highest mountain up a breathtaking right of way with grades as steep as 37.41%. The average grade is 25% to summit of Mt. Washington, elevation 6288 ft.

Schedule: May 23 through mid-October, hourly service each day from 9:00 A.M. Rain or shine. Minimum load required. Last train 3 hours before sunset. All trains subject to cancellation due to lack of passengers or weather conditions.

Fare: Reservations strongly recommended. Round trip to summit, shuttle ride from parking area and museum admission, $25.00. Shuttle and museum only, $3.00. Descent only, $15.00. Group rates available. Call for reservations.

Locomotives: Eight 0-2-2-0 cog wheel locomotives with inclined boilers. Seven of these engines built by Manchester Locomotive Works between 1870 and 1908. Locomotive #10, "Col. Teague" was built in the Mt. Washington shops in 1972. A new locomotive, #8, constructed in our shops, was placed in service in 1983.

Train: Open or closed platform coach.

Displays: "Old Peppersass," the world's first cog engine, on display at Base Station. Museum with historical exhibits and audio-visual presentation.

Joel Bedor, President

✔Refreshments
✔Gift Shop
✔Picnic Area
✔Restaurant

Mount Washington Railway Co.
Mt. Washington, NH 03589
Phone (603) 846-5404
For reservations, toll-free
1-800-922-8825

**Conway
Scenic Railroad**

Steam, scheduled
Standard gauge

Photo by D. T. Walker

Location: The depot faces the village park in North Conway, a resort town on Routes 16 and 302 in New Hampshire's Mt. Washington Valley.

Ride: An 11-mile, 55-minute round trip from North Conway to Conway over trackage first laid down in 1872. The train travels through farmlands in the Saco River Valley with views of forests and mountains.

Schedule: Daily operation, June 13 thru October 25. Week-ends, May 2 to June 7 plus Memorial Day. Trains depart 11:00 A.M., 1:00, 2:30 & 4:00 P.M. "Sunset Special" departs at 7:00 P.M. Tuesdays, Wednesdays, Thursdays and Saturdays during July and August. Annual Railfan's Day, Saturday, September 19, 1987. Winter trips, November 27-29 at 1:30 P.M.

Fare: Adults $5.00, Children $3.00, under 4 free.
Group rates available.

Locomotives: #47, 0-6-0, Grand Trunk (1921), ex-Canadian National.
#108, 2-6-2, Baldwin (1920), ex-Reader R.R.
#501, 2-8-0, Alco (1910), ex-Maine Central R.R. (Display).
#15, 44-ton diesel, General Electric (1945), ex-Maine Central.
#1055, S-4 diesel, Alco-G.E. (1950), ex-Portland Terminal Co.
#4266, F-7 diesel, E.M.D. (1949), ex-Boston & Maine.

Train: Coaches and open observation cars.

Displays: A museum of railroad memorabilia is located within the ornate 113 year-old passenger depot. An old-time roundhouse and operating turntable highlight the railroad yard which also features many pieces of railroad rolling stock on display. The facilities of Conway Scenic R.R. are in the National Register of Historic Places.

Dwight A. Smith, President & General Manager

✔Refreshments
✔Gift Shop
✔Picnic Area

Conway Scenic Railroad, Inc.
P.O. Box 947
North Conway, NH 03860
Phone (603) 356-5251

Steam, scheduled
36" gauge

Photo by Jean-David Beyer

Location: The New Jersey Museum of Transportation operates the Pine Creek Railroad at Allaire State Park, Route 524, Wall Township, Monmouth County, a short distance west of Garden State Parkway Exit 98 and 1 mile east of I-95, Exit 31.

Ride: A 10-minute, 1½-mile ride over a loop track in the park.

Schedule: STEAM: Saturdays, Sundays & Holidays, mid-April through mid-October. DIESEL: Week-days, July & August. Trains leave every 30 minutes, Noon to 5:00 P.M.

Fare: Adults, Children $1.00, under 3 free. Members free.
Christmas Express, $1.50 per person.

Locomotives: #6, 2-truck Shay, Lima (1927), ex-Ely-Thomas Lumber Co.; #3L, "Lady Edith", 4-4-0T, Stephenson (1887), ex-Cavan & Leitram Ry. (Ireland); #26, 2-6-2, Baldwin (1920), ex-Surry, Sussex & Southampton Ry.; #1, 12-ton diesel, Plymouth (1942), ex-Haws Refractories; #40, 25-ton diesel, Whitcomb (1940), ex-Midvale Steel Corp.; #7751, 25-ton diesel, General Electric (1942), ex-U.S. Army.

Train: Newfoundland Ry. open platform wood coach #502 (1902), open excursion car, C.N.J. wood caboose #91155 (1874).

Displays: A variety of narrow gauge engines and cars are either on display or being restored in the railroad's shop. Allaire Park is the site of a restored iron-making community of the early 1800's.

Special Events: Civil War Re-enactment, June 21. Railroader's Day, September 13. Christmas Express runs December 5-6, 12-13, 19-20, 1987. Noon to 3:00 P.M.

✔Refreshments
✔Gift Shop
✔Picnic Area
✔Camping
✔Memberships

TRAIN

New Jersey Museum of Transportation
P.O. Box 622
Farmingdale, NJ 07727
Phone (201) 938-5524

NEW JERSEY, RINGOES-FLEMINGTON
Black River & Western R.R.

Steam, scheduled
Standard gauge

Photo by John E. Helbok

Location: Ringoes depot is located on County Route 579, ¾-mile from the junction of Highways 202 and 31. At Flemington the depot is in the center of town near Liberty Village.

Ride: The train trip takes 1 hour and runs from Ringoes to Flemington and return. Running on a former branch of the Pennsylvania R.R. the traveler passes through some of New Jersey's most scenic farm country. Passengers may board the train at either Ringoes or Flemington.

Schedule: Saturdays, Sundays & Holidays, April 18 thru November 29, 1987.
Lv. Ringoes	10:45	12:15	1:45	3:15	4:45
Lv. Flemington	11:30	1:00	2:30	4:00	5:30*

Tuesdays through Fridays, July through Labor Day:
Lv. Ringoes	12:30	1:30	2:30	3:30
Lv. Flemington	1:00	2:00	3:00	4:00*

*One-way trip
Note: Week-day trips will be operated with ex-Pennsylvania R.R. Gas-Electric Car #4666.

Fare: Round trip: Adults $6.00, Children (5-12) $3.00,Children (3-4) $1.00, under 3 free.

Locomotives: #60, 2-8-0, Alco (1937), ex-Great Western Ry.

Train: Coaches and combine from the Jersey Central and Lackawanna and two open excursion cars.

Displays: At Flemington don't miss Turntable Junction and Liberty Village, old-time shops and outlet stores adjacent to the B.R.&W. depot.

✔Refreshments
✔Gift Shop
✔Picnic Area

Black River & Western R.R.
P.O. Box 200
Ringoes, NJ 08551
Phone (201) 782-9600

Photo by Bob Pennisi

Location: The Museum is located at 1 Railroad Plaza at the junction of Route 10 and Whippany Road in Morris County.

Displays: The Whippany Railway Museum is located in the restored 1904 freight house of the Morristown & Erie Railway and is the only museum in the North Jersey area devoted exclusively to railroading. Inside are displays and artifacts from many area railroads including headlights, bells, whistles, photos, tickets and a large Lionel "O" gauge layout. On display outdoors are a number of privately owned pieces of railroad rolling stock, many of which are in the process of restoration.

Schedule: Open Sundays, April through October, from Noon to 4:00 P.M.

Admission: Donation.

Locomotives: Ex-Bangor & Aroostook F-3 diesel #44, owned by Tri-State Chapter, N.R.H.S.

Rolling Stock: Ex-Lackawanna electric coaches, Erie Stillwell coach, cabooses from D.&H., Erie, C.N.J., L.&N.E., D.L.&W., E-L, Raritan River and B.A.R.

At the Morristown & Erie's shop is Tri-State Chapter's ex-Jersey Central "Blue Comet" observation car "Tempel" and the M.&E.'s business car, ex-Erie #1, both being restored.

Note: Tri-State Chapter's ex-E-L Safety & Training Car #10, displayed at Whippany, is occasionally open to the public and features many interesting displays.

✔Gift Shop
✔Picnic Area
✔Memberships

Whippany Railway Museum
P.O. Box 16
Whippany, NJ 07981

115

NEW MEXICO, CHAMA
COLORADO, ANTONITO
Cumbres & Toltec Scenic R.R.

Steam, scheduled

36" gauge

Location: Trains leave from terminals at Chama, NM and Antonito, CO.

Ride: Steam trains travel over highly scenic ex-Denver & Rio Grande Western narrow-gauge trackage. The 64-mile line crosses Cumbres Pass (elevation 10,015 ft.), goes through the spectacular Toltec Gorge, over high bridges and through two tunnels. Passengers may choose either the COLORADO LIMITED from Antonito to Osier via Toltec Gorge, or the NEW MEXICO EXPRESS from Chama to Osier via Cumbres Pass. The two trains meet at Osier, Colo. for a lunch stop and the trains exchange locomotives for the return trip.

Schedule: Trains operate Daily from mid-June thru mid-October. Lv. Chama 10:30 A.M., return 4:30 P.M. Lv. Antonito 10:00 A.M., return 5:00 P.M.

Fare: Round-trip fares on either train: Adults $27.00, Children (11 & under) $10.00. Reservations recommended, may be made by mail or phone. Also available are through trips from either terminal with return by van. Adults $41.50, Children $20.00. Overnight specials from $121.00 each, double occupancy for Adults, $55.00 for Children. Single occupancy $131.00.

Locomotives: #484, 487, 488, 489, 2-8-2, Baldwin (1925), ex-D.&R.G.W.

Train: Coaches, snack bar, souvenir shop car, open observation car. Note: Due to the sudden and dramatic changes in the weather, passengers are advised to dress warmly.

Note: The C.&T.S.R.R. is a joint undertaking of the States of Colorado and New Mexico. The line is a Registered National Historical Site and is leased to Kyle Railways, Inc.

R. D. Ranger, General Manager

✔Refreshments
✔Gift Shop
✔Midway lunch stop

TRAIN

Cumbres & Toltec Scenic R.R.
P.O. Box 789   P.O. Box 668
Chama, NM 87520   Antonito, CO 81120
Phone (505) 756-2151 Phone (303) 376-5483

Photo by George A. Forero, Jr.

Location: Arcade is located in the western part of New York State, midway between Buffalo and Olean. Trains depart from the Arcade & Attica depot in the center of town, where Route 39 joins Route 98.

Ride: A 15-mile, 1½-hour round trip over the historic Arcade & Attica R.R. to Curriers and return. This is a common-carrier railroad, which has been in existence since 1881.

Schedule: Steam train operates Saturdays, Sundays & Holidays, May 23 to October 31, 1987. Train also operates Wednesdays during July and August. Train leaves depot at Arcade at Noon, 2:00 & 4:00 P.M.

Fare: Adults $5.00, Children $3.00, under 3 free.
Group rates available for parties of 25 or more.

Locomotives: #14, 4-6-0, Baldwin (1917), ex-Escanaba & Lake Superior. #18, 2-8-0, Alco, Cooke (1920), ex-Boyne City R.R.

Train: Open end steel coaches and combines from the Lackawanna R.R. and open gondola cars.

Displays: New York, Ontario & Western Ry. wooden business car #30 is on display at Arcade. This historic car may be visited on passenger train operating days. The N.Y.O. & W. Ry. ceased operations in 1957.

✔Gift Shop
✔Picnic Area
✔Refreshments

Arcade & Attica R.R.
278 Main Street
Arcade, NY 14009
Phone (716) 496-9877

Location: Arkville is located in the heart of New York's Catskill Mountains. Take the N.Y. State Thruway to Exit 19, (Kingston) and drive 43 miles west on Route 28. From the Route 17 Quickway, take Route 30 north at East Branch to Route 28.

Ride: A choice of two trips over the route of the historic Ulster & Delaware R.R. A 14-mile, 1¼-hour round trip from Arkville to Highmount or a 14-mile, 1¼-hour round trip from Arkville to Halcottsville.

Schedule: Week-ends, May 23 through November 1. Wednesdays through Sundays, July 1 through September 8. Trains depart from Arkville depot at 10:30 A.M., 12:15, 2:00 & 3:45 P.M. Destinations alternate with the first train going to Halcottsville.

Fare: Adults $5.00, Children (5-11) $2.50, age 4 and under free.

Locomotives: M-405, diesel-electric railcar, J.G. Brill Co. (1928), ex-New York Central. #76, 44-ton diesel, General Electric (1943), ex-Western Maryland. #1012, S-4 diesel, Alco (1955), ex-Ford Motor Co.

Train: Brill railcar "The Red Heifer" may operate with matching Brill trailer car. The original "Red Heifer" was the Brill car which operated on the Delaware & Northern R.R. out of Arkville from 1927 to 1942. Locomotive powered trains operate with P.R.R. MP-54 coaches, open cars, P.R.R. caboose.

Displays: The Arkville depot opens at 10:00 A.M. on operating days, features a free slide show, model railroad and railway exhibits.

Charles A. Christiansen, General Manager

✔Refreshments
✔Gift Shop
✔Picnic Area
✔Free Parking

Delaware & Ulster Rail Ride
Route 28
Arkville, NY 12406
Phone (914) 586-DURR
New York State Phone 1-800-356-5615
Northeast Region 1-800-642-4443

NEW YORK, GOWANDA
New York & Lake Erie R.R.

Diesel, scheduled
Standard gauge

Photo by Fred B. Furminger

Location: Trains leave from 50 Commercial St. in Gowanda in western New York. Gowanda is on U.S. Route 62 and State 39, 26 miles south of Buffalo.

Ride: A 20-mile, 2-hour round trip from Gowanda to South Dayton and back over a steep grade and through an old stone tunnel. This trackage was part of the Erie Railroad's Jamestown to Buffalo line. Longer special trips operate to Salamanca, stopping at the Salamanca Rail Museum, former depot of the B.R.&P.R.R.

Schedule: Regular train operates Saturdays and Sundays only, June through November 1, 1987. Also runs Memorial Day and Labor Day. Train departs Gowanda at 1:00 and 3:30 P.M.
Special runs operate on selected Saturdays, write for dates.
Group charters available.

Fare: Adults $6.00, Children $4.00, under 3 free.
Longer 7 to 9 hour, 60 and 90 mile special trips, write for fares.

Locomotives: #75, S-2 diesel, Alco (1947), ex-South Buffalo Ry.
#1013, C-425 diesel, Alco (1965), ex-Norfolk & Western Ry.

Train: Three former Baltimore & Ohio coaches, restored. Three former D.L.&W. electric commuter cars, one ex-Amtrak (NKP) coach and one open-air car.

Displays: #1700, General Electric center-cab diesel, built in 1940 for the Ford Motor Co., later used on the Wellsville, Addison & Galeton R.R.

✔Refreshments
✔Gift Shop

New York & Lake Erie R.R.
50 Commercial St.
Gowanda, NY 14070
Phone (716) 532-5242

NEW YORK, KINGSTON

Trolley Museum of New York

Electric Railway Museum
Scheduled Rides
Standard gauge

Location: The Trolley Museum of New York is located in the historic East Strand area of Kingston on the Rondout Creek waterfront. The site is opposite the Kingston Maritime Museum. This section of Kingston is being restored to its original late 19th century appearance.

Ride: A 2½-mile, 40-minute round trip from the foot of Broadway to Kingston Point with stops at the Museum in both directions. Self-propelled railcar operates on private right-of-way and in-street trackage along Rondout Creek to the Hudson River. Trackage was once part of the Ulster & Delaware R.R.'s main-line.

Schedule: Saturdays, Sundays & Holidays from May 23 through October 12. Daily operation, July 3 through September 7. Museum open Noon to 5:00 P.M. Trips leave every hour on the hour. Additional trips as necessary. Week-day group trips by advance arrangement.

Fare: Adults $1.00 per trip, Children (12 and under) 50¢ per trip, under 4 free.

Railcar: #120, gasoline-powered railcar, Brill (1919), ex-Remington Rand, ex-Sperry Rail Service.

Trolleys: 2 Hudson & Manhattan subway cars, 3 Boston trolleys, 1 Brussels trolley, 1 Hamburg trolley. Other pieces of subway, trolley and railroad equipment are being moved to the site as space and finances permit. Staten Island #508 renovated as gift shop and ticket office.

✔Refreshments
✔Gift Shop
✔Picnic Area
✔Memberships

Trolley Museum of New York
89 East Strand
Kingston, NY 12401
Phone (914) 331-3399

NEW YORK, MARTISCO
Martisco Station Museum

Railway Museum
Standard gauge

Location: Martisco Station Museum is located in the former New York Central passenger station at Martisco, off Route 174, five miles west of Syracuse.

Displays: The 1870 station, restored to museum condition by the Central New York Chapter of the National Railway Historical Society, features extensive displays of railroadiana, photographs and a comprehensive library located in a former Penn Central dining car, adjacent to the building. In addition, four railroad passenger cars are displayed at the New York State Fairgrounds at Solvay, four miles east.

Schedule: The museum is open Sundays, May through October from 2:00 to 5:00 P.M. Other times by appointment. Passenger cars, including interior exhibits, are open to visitors daily during the New York State Fair, held last week of August.

Admission: Free, but donations are welcomed.

Equipment: The Chapter owns the ex-James E. Strates Shows' 1929 private car "Syracuse", formerly Pullman solarium sleeper "Palm Lane"; Baltimore & Ohio dormitory parlor-diner #1302, a Long Island electric MU coach, R.F.&P. 54-seat coach #804 and Delaware & Hudson coach #229. Also, Boston & Maine R.R. F-7A diesel #4265, Amtrak GG-1 #4926 and New York Central Alco RS-3 #8223.

✔Gift Shop
✔Memberships

Martisco Station Museum
Central New York Chapter, N.R.H.S.
P.O. Box 229
Marcellus, NY 13108
Phone (315) 672-8063

 Syracuse

Photo by John Prestopino

Location: The Catskill Mountain R.R. operates over trackage of the former Ulster & Delaware R.R., later the Catskill Mountain branch of the New York Central. Take the New York State Thruway to Kingston (Exit 19) and travel west on Route 28 for 22 miles to Mt. Pleasant.

Ride: A 6-mile, ¾-hour round trip from Mt. Pleasant to Phoenicia along scenic Esopus Creek. Tourists, tubers, canoers and fishermen may ride one-way or round-trip. The train travels through the heart of the beautiful Catskill Mountains. Passengers may return immediately or stop at Phoenicia to visit shops or restaurants and return on a later train.

Schedule: Saturdays, Sundays & Holidays, May 23 through September 13. Trains operate 11:00 A.M. to 5:00 P.M. Call for Fall Foliage Specials and other special events.

Fare: Adults: $4.00 round-trip, $3.00 one-way. Children (4-11) $1.00, under 4 free.

Locomotives: #1, "The Duck", 38-ton diesel-mechanical, Davenport (1942), ex-U.S. Air Force.

Train: Open flatcars, Delaware & Hudson wooden caboose.

Displays: Wooden baggage car, ex-Delaware & Hudson, built 1894. Gift-shop caboose, ex-Lehigh Valley #94071, built 1937.

Other Equipment: #2361, RS-1 diesel, Alco (1952), ex-Wisconsin Central (Soo Line).
#8301, self-propelled diesel crane (1942), ex-U.S. Army.

✔Refreshments
✔Gift Shop
✔Picnic Area
✔Campsites nearby
✔Tourist information

TRAIN

Catskill Mountain Railroad
P.O. Box 46
Shokan, NY 12481
Phone (914) 688-7400

NEW YORK, NEW YORK
New York City Transit Exhibit

Photo by New York City Transit Authority

Location: The Transit Exhibit is located in the former Court St. Station in Brooklyn. This station, which has been closed for many years, is 2 blocks south of Brooklyn's Borough Hall. The entrance is at the corner of Boerum Place and Schermerhorn Street.

Displays: A number of old subway cars, in their original colors and with their original fixtures, are displayed in a vintage subway station. The setting is perfect, the cars and station are spotless and well maintained. Included in the display are the old IRT low-voltage type; a BMT standard; Car #100, first car built for the IND system and a BMT elevated car, among others. In addition to the cars, there is a display of old-time fare collection devices, pictures, models, signs, badges and other memorabilia.

Schedule: Open Daily, 9:30 A.M. to 4:00 P.M.

Admission: Adults, 1 token ($1.00), 17 years and under, 50¢.

Note: The Transit Exhibit will be undergoing remodeling work this year, but is expected to remain open.

Camille Akeju, Museum Specialist

New York City Transit Authority
370 Jay Street - Rm. #816
Brooklyn, NY 11201
Phone (212) 330-3060
(212) 330-3063

 New York

NEW YORK, OWEGO
Tioga Central Rail Excursions

Diesel, scheduled
Standard gauge

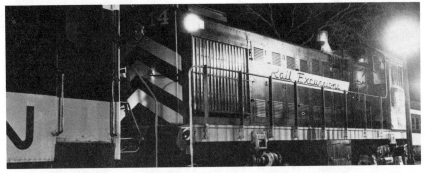

Photo by Tom Shade

Location: Tioga Central trains operate from the Tioga Transportation Museum at Flemingville, 5 miles north of Owego on N.Y. Rt. 38. The site is just north of the Route 17 expressway along New York's Southern Tier.

Ride: Trains operate an 11-mile, 1¼-hour round trip or a 40-mile, 3-hour round trip over the former Lehigh Valley R.R.'s Auburn Branch. On the 11-mile "Museum Trail" they may stop off for visits to 3 museums. The "Evening Express" and "Morning Star" offer a 3-hour round trip to North Harford with dining car service available.

Schedule: May 1 through December 22: "The Museum Trail" departs Saturdays & Sundays at 12:00, 1:30, 3:00 & 4:30 P.M. "The Evening Express" departs Friday and Saturday at 7:00 P.M. (dining reservations required). "The Morning Star" leaves Saturday at 9:00 A.M. All departures are from Flemingville Station.

Fare: "The Museum Trail": Adults $4.50, Children (6-12) $2.50, under 6 free. "The Evening Express": rail fare $10.00, dining additional. "The Morning Star": rail fare Adults $8.00, Children (6-12) $4.00, breakfast extra.

Locomotives: #14, S-2 diesel, Alco (1947), ex-Buffalo Creek R.R.; #47 & #62, RS-1 diesels, Alco (1950), ex-Washington Terminal Co.; #12, 0-4-0, Vulcan (1918), ex-Dexter & Northern R.R.

Rolling Stock: Coaches #233, ex-Delaware & Hudson; #5212 & 5285, ex-Canadian National; #71 & 78, ex-Pennsylvania R.R. Observation car #300, ex-Adirondack R.R.; Dining cars #1372, ex-VIA & #372, ex-P.R.R.

Displays: At Flemingville, the restored station, built in 1902, is a working example of a rural Lehigh Valley depot. The Carriage House features a collection of over 50 carriages, antique autos, bicycles and other unusual vehicles. Also visit the Newark Valley Depot Museum and the Bement-Billings Farmstead.

✔Refreshments
✔Gift Shop
✔Picnic Area
✔Dining Cars
✔Memberships

Tioga Central Rail Excursions
R.D. #4, Box 4240, Route 38
Owego, NY 13827
Phone (607) 642-5511

Photo by Paul Monte

Location: The Museum is located on East River Road, 2 miles south of the New York State Thruway (Exit 46) about 15 minutes from the city of Rochester.

Displays: This comprehensive museum has preserved a number of transportation artifacts from New York State and elsewhere. There is an 1867 Rochester horsecar; Rochester & Eastern interurban car #157 (1914); Philadelphia snow-sweeper C-130; Genesee & Wyoming R.R. wooden caboose #8; several busses and antique automobiles. Under restoration are a Plymouth gasoline locomotive and several trolleys. There is also a collection of railroad memorabilia located in the Museum.

Schedule: Museum is open Sundays only, year-round. Hours are 11:00 A.M. to 4:00 P.M.

Admission: Adults $1.00, Children (under 12) 50¢.

Operations: A loop of trackage encircles the Museum site and is being extended as time and weather permit. Track construction will be underway during all of the 1987 season.

Note: The Museum plans to extend its trackage to the site of the adjoining Oatka Depot, so that there will be a rail display at each end of the line.

✔Refreshments
✔Gift Shop
✔Memberships

New York Museum of Transportation
P.O. Box 136
West Henrietta, NY 14586
Phone (716) 533-1113

Rochester

Location: The Depot is located on Route 251 at 282 Rush-Scottsville Road, a short distance south of the city of Rochester.

Displays: The Museum is housed in a restored 1900 vintage Erie Railroad station. The restoration was begun in 1969 and has now been completed. Inside the depot are railroad artifacts from area railroads.

On outdoor display tracks are a number of railroad cars and plans are underway to complete the trackage between the Oatka Depot and the New York Museum of Transportation. When completed, this will afford a 4-mile round trip between the adjoining sites.

Locomotives: #6, 80-ton diesel, G.E. (1946), ex-Eastman Kodak Co.
#211, RS-3m diesel, Alco, ex-Lehigh Valley.

Rolling Stock: #633, Baltimore & Ohio steel baggage car; B.&O. caboose C-2631, Erie caboose C-254; #2328, Erie Stillwell coach; #4628, Lackawanna MU car; New York Central flat car; the "Poquott"/"Pine Falls", an ex-L.I.R.R./P.R.R. tavern-lounge car, Pullman (1940) and Erie-Lackawanna steel baggage car #489022.

Schedule: Open Sundays only, Memorial Day through October from 1:00 to 5:00 P.M.

Admission: Adults $1.00, Children (5-12) 50¢, under 5 free.
Family maximum $5.00.

Note: The Museum is a project of the Rochester Chapter, National Railway Historical Society. 1987 marks the Chapter's 50th Anniversary.

🖊Gift Shop
🖊Memberships

Oatka Depot Railroad Museum
P.O. Box 664
Rochester, NY 14603
Phone (716) 533-1431

 Rochester

Location: Located midway between Boone and Blowing Rock on U.S. 221-321. Exit Blue Ridge Parkway at Mile Post 291.

Ride: Tweetsie Railroad operates a 3-mile, 25-minute loop trip in conjunction with a re-created Western town. Indian raids, train hold-ups featured on each run.

Schedule: Daily, Memorial Day week-end through the end of October. Steam train operates from 9:00 A.M. to 6:00 P.M.

Fare: General Admission (includes train ride and other attractions): Adults $9.00, Children $7.00, under 4 free.

Locomotives: #12, 4-6-0, Baldwin (1917), ex-East Tennessee & Western North Carolina R.R. #190, 2-8-2, Baldwin (1943), ex-White Pass & Yukon Ry.

Train: Open excursion cars, wooden combine, coach.

Displays: Tweetsie R.R. is an old-time railroad theme park in the high country of North Carolina. Enjoy live entertainment at the Tweetsie Palace. An 1890's general store, petting farm, Country Fair with rides and arcade and various gift, refreshment and souvenir shops are also located in the park.

✔Refreshments
✔Gift Shop
✔Picnic Area
✔Restaurant
✔Lodging

Tweetsie Railroad
P.O. Box 388
Blowing Rock, NC 28605
Phone (704) 264-9061

Photo by Wes Miller

Location: Spencer is just off I-85 about 3 miles north of Salisbury. The Shops are at 411 S. Salisbury Ave. (U.S. 29-70) in downtown Spencer. The location is on the main-line of the former Southern Railway, now Norfolk Southern, and is still an important railroad center.

Displays: Spencer Shops was the largest railroad repair facility on the Southern Railway. Over 2500 people were employed in the various portions of the vast 57-acre complex. The massive Back Shop, 37-stall roundhouse and nine other major buildings are being restored to chronicle the history of transportation in the State of North Carolina. A Visitor's Center has been established in the Master Mechanic's Office. Exhibits are displayed in the former Warehouse Building.

Admission: No charge. Donations accepted.

Schedule: April 1-October 31: Daily, 9:00 A.M. to 5:00 P.M. except Sundays, 1:00 to 5:00 P.M.
November 1-March 31: Daily, except closed Mondays, 10:00 A.M. to 4:00 P.M., Sundays, 1:00 to 4:00 P.M. Closed on major holidays. Hours subject to change.

Operation: Steam train rides are expected to begin in mid-1987. Train will be powered by locomotive #4, 2-8-0, Baldwin (1926), ex-Southwest Virginia. This engine has been restored by Southern Ry. retirees for use at Spencer Shops.

Exhibits: The exhibit "People, Places and Times" traces the development of transportation and features artifacts from an Indian canoe and Conestoga wagon to a Model AA Ford truck and a Skyranger airplane. Railroad rolling stock on display includes a baggage car and passenger coach. Also a refrigerator car, boxcar and Seaboard caboose. A multi-image program "From Here To There" is shown inside a refrigerator car converted into a theater. Spencer Shops has been placed on the National Register of Historic Places.

✔Refreshments
✔Museum Shop
✔Picnic Area
✔Memberships

Spencer Shops State Historic Site
P.O. Box 165
Spencer, NC 28159
Phone (704) 636-2889

 Salisbury

Location: The Museum is located in the former Atlantic Coast Line Freight Office and Warehouse A at Red Cross & North Water Sts. in Wilmington.

Displays: The Museum building was built in 1876 by the Wilmington & Weldon R.R., enlarged by the Atlantic Coast Line, and abandoned in 1973. Outside, 1 of only 4 remaining ACL steam locomotives is on display, as well as an Atlantic Coast Line caboose. Within the Museum are many unique railroad artifacts donated by area residents. Included is a collection of railroad dining car china, a 1941 Fairmont track speeder and an extensive collection of maintenance-of-way tools. The station bell on the front lawn was cast in Philadelphia in 1855. It used to toll 5 minutes before the departure of each train.

Schedule: Open Tuesday through Saturday from 10:00 A.M. to 5:00 P.M., Sundays from 1:00 to 5:00 P.M. year-round. Closed Mondays. Group tours welcome, please call phone number below.

Admission: No charge. Donations welcome.

Locomotives: On display is #250, 4-6-0, Baldwin (1910), ex-A.C.L.

Rolling Stock: Caboose No. 01983, Atlantic Coast Line.

Note: Wilmington Railroad Museum is located on the east bank of the Cape Fear River. A few blocks away is Riverfront Park where the battleship U.S.S. North Carolina is moored.

✔Gift Shop   Wilmington Railroad Museum
✔Picnic Area   P.O. Box 4674
✔Memberships   Wilmington, NC 28406
                                            Phone (919) 763-2634

Location: 243 Southwest St., 2 blocks south of downtown Bellevue.

Displays: Numerous railway displays and exhibits can be found in the various cabooses, freight cars and buildings in the museum complex.

Schedule: Museum is open Tuesdays through Sundays during June, July & August. Open Saturdays & Sundays in May and September, Sundays only in October. Hours are 1:00 to 5:00 P.M. Special tours by appointment.

Admission: No charge. Donations accepted.

Locomotives: #7, 0-6-0, Porter (1943) fireless, ex-Cleveland Electric.
#671, restored F-7A diesel, E.M.D. (Canada), ex-Wabash R.R.
#740, H-12-44 diesel, Fairbanks-Morse, ex-Milwaukee Road.
#1190, 0-6-0, Brooks (1904), ex-B.R.&P. R.R.
#329, RSD-12 diesel, Alco, ex-Nickel Plate Road.

Passenger Cars: #4714, C.B.&Q. "Silver Dome"; #105, Nickel Plate coach; #618, Milwaukee Road coach; #1484, L.&N. baggage-express car; #1375, N.&W. baggage car; heavyweight Pullman sleeper "Donizetti"; #6102, Seaboard dining car; #6570, Pennsylvania R.R. R.P.O. car; #3479, Santa Fe baggage-dormitory car.

Rolling Stock: On hand at the Museum is a large and diverse collection of cabooses, freight cars and maintenance-of-way equipment.

Dennis Brandal, Curator

✔Excursions
✔Gift Shop
✔Picnic Area
✔Memberships

TRAIN

Mad River & NKP Railroad Museum
P.O. Box 42
Bellevue, OH 44811
Phone (419) 483-2222

 Sandusky

Photo by David R. Hanna

Location: Train departs from parking area about 2 blocks from the intersection of I-77 and Rockside Road in the Cleveland suburb of Independence.

Ride: A 55-mile, 7-hour round trip thru the scenic Cuyahoga Valley National Recreation Area to Akron, including a visit to Quaker Square, a converted Quaker Oats factory which now houses over 40 shops and restaurants. Passengers may elect to detrain at Hale Farm & Village, a 19th century restoration, for a 4½-hour visit. Entrance fee additional.

Schedule: Train operates Saturdays, August 1 through October 31. Will also operate a number of Sundays, write for dates. Leaves Independence 11:00 A.M., returns 6:00 P.M. Stops at Hale Farm at Noon, arrives Akron 12:45 P.M. Leaves Akron 4:00 P.M., Hale Farm 4:30 P.M.

Fare: Cleveland/Akron: Adults $17.95, Children $9.95, 1st Class $27.95. Lower fares apply Cleveland/Hale Farm and Hale Farm/Akron. Reservations recommended. MasterCard/Visa/AmEx cards accepted. Write for complete schedules and fares.

Locomotives: #4070, 2-8-2, Alco (1918), ex-Grand Trunk Western. This locomotive is owned by the Midwest Railway Historical Foundation. Cuyahoga Valley Line reserves the right to substitute other equipment for the engine and rolling stock when necessary.

Train: Railway Post Office, coaches and Pullman cars owned by the Midwest Railway Historical Foundation. Completely restored Pullman lounge car "Mount Baxter" available at charter rates.

✔Refreshments on train
✔Gift Shop on train
✔Memberships

 Cleveland

Cuyahoga Valley Line
P.O. Box 502
Sagamore Hills, OH 44067
Phone Cleveland (216) 468-0797
Akron (216) 650-9504

Photo by Paul W. Prescott

Location: The Conneaut Railroad Museum is located in the old New York Central station on Depot and Mill Sts., north of U.S. 20 and I-90. Our blue and white locomotive signs point the way to the Museum.

Displays: The station was built by the Lake Shore & Michigan Southern in 1900 and is adjacent to the Conrail (NYC) tracks. Inside are large displays of timetables, passes, lanterns, old photos, builder's plates, telegraph instruments and models of locos, cars and structures. An HO scale model railroad is on display with week-end operation. On display outside, in addition to the train are section cars, track equipment and an old ball signal. On the station platform are baggage trucks, hand carts and old trunks. A steady parade of Conrail trains pass in review for the railfans and other visitors.

Schedule: Open Daily, Memorial Day through Labor Day from Noon to 5:00 P.M.

Admission: No charge but donations are welcome.

Equipment: #755, 2-8-4, Lima (1944), ex-Nickel Plate Road.
Bessemer & Lake Erie 90-ton hopper car.
Bessemer & Lake Erie wooden caboose.

✔Gift Shop
✔Picnic Area
✔Memberships

Conneaut Railroad Museum
P.O. Box 643
Conneaut, OH 44030
Phone (216) 599-7878

Location: Mason is in southwest Ohio, a short distance north of Cincinnati. Take U.S. 42, Reading Road, from Cincinnati. The train leaves from Forest and Western Avenues in Mason.

Ride: A 16-mile, 2-hour round trip through the rolling hills of southwest Ohio. The line over which the train passes was once a branch of the Pennsylvania Railroad and later Conrail. Passengers may leave the train at scheduled stops and reboard a later train.

Schedule: Saturdays, Sundays & Holidays, May 23 through November 1, 1987. Trains leave Mason at Noon, 2:00 & 4:00 P.M.

Fare: Adults $7.00, Children $3.50, under 2 free.

Locomotives: #51, GP-7 diesel, E.M.D. (1949), ex-Burlington Route.

Train: 4 electric commuter cars built in 1930 for the Delaware, Lackawanna & Western R.R. These cars were used in continuous commuter service until 1984.

Note: The Indiana & Ohio R.R. is a common-carrier freight and passenger railroad.

Mailing Address:

✓Refreshments
✓Picnic Area

 Cincinnati

Indiana & Ohio Railroad
11020 Reading Road (Suite 501)
Cincinnati, OH 45241
Phone (513) 777-5777

Photo by Michael A. Eagleson

Location: Nelsonville is located in southeastern Ohio, about 40 miles east of Columbus on Route 33. Trains leave from depot on Route 33 and Hocking Parkway in Nelsonville.

Ride: A choice of two trips are offered each operating day. A 10-mile round trip to Diamond with a visit to Hocking Tech Forestry Museum or a 25-mile round trip to Logan. The train operates over a former Chesapeake & Ohio route that was once a part of the original Hocking Valley Ry.

Schedule: Saturdays, Sundays and major Holidays, May 30 through November 1, 1987. Train to Diamond leaves at Noon, to Logan leaves 2:00 P.M. Annual Santa Claus train runs first three week-ends in December.

Fare: To Diamond: Adults $5.00, Children $3.00.
To Logan: Adults $9.00, Children $5.00.

Locomotives: #33, 2-8-0, Baldwin (1916), ex-Lake Superior & Ishpeming.
#5833, GP-7 diesel, E.M.D. (1952), ex-Chesapeake & Ohio.
#7318, diesel, General Electric (1942), ex-U.S. Army.
#3, 0-6-0, Baldwin (1920) (under restoration).

Train: Rock Island and Erie R.R. coaches, Baltimore & Ohio combination car, open-air car.

✔Refreshments
✔Gift Shop
✔Picnic Area
✔Memberships

Hocking Valley Scenic Railway
P.O. Box 427
Nelsonville, OH 45764
Phone (513) 335-0382
(614) 753-9531 (Week-ends during operating season)

OHIO, NEWARK
Buckeye Central Scenic R.R.

Diesel, scheduled
Standard gauge

Location: The Buckeye Central Scenic R.R. is located near Newark, in central Ohio. Trains depart from the National Road Station on State Route 40. The station is between Jacksontown and Hebron and is one mile north of Interstate 70.

Ride: A 10-mile, 1-hour round trip over a portion of the old Shawnee Branch of the Baltimore & Ohio R.R. The diesel-powered train passes through central Ohio countryside, over 2 trestles and a bridge.

Schedule: Train operates Saturdays, Sundays and Holidays from Memorial Day week-end through the end of October. Departure times are 1:00 & 3:00 P.M. Annual Christmas runs held the first two week-ends in December. Special charter trips available.

Fare: Adults $3.00, Children (3-11) $2.00, Golden Buckeye Cardholders receive 50¢ discount.

Locomotives: #8599, SW-1 diesel, E.M.D. (1948), ex-B.&O.R.R.

Train: Former Baltimore & Ohio open air coaches, gondola and caboose.

George Beckett, President

✔Refreshments
✔Gift Shop
✔Memberships

Buckeye Central Scenic R.R.
P.O. Box 242
Newark, OH 43055
Phone (614) 349-8312

OHIO, OLMSTED TOWNSHIP
Gerald E. Brookins Museum of Electric Railways, Inc.
Trolleyville, U.S.A.

Electric, scheduled

Standard gauge

Location: The Museum is located in Olmsted Township at 7100 Columbia Road, State Route 252, east of Exit 9 of the Ohio Turnpike, 6 miles west of I-71 (Bagley Road exit) and 2 miles south of I-480 (Great Northern exit).

Ride: A 2½-mile ride over a scenic route and a ride into the carbarn to view the rest of the cars.

Schedule: Sundays & Holidays from Memorial Day through the end of September, 1:00 to 6:00 p.m. Also Wednesdays and Fridays during June, July & August, 10:00 A.M. to 3:00 P.M.

Fare: Adults $1.75, Children under 12, $1.25. Group charters available Monday through Friday, April through October.

Trolleys: Brill-built Vera Cruz open summer trolleys; Chicago, Aurora & Elgin heavyweight and Aurora, Elgin & Fox River lightweight interurbans. Also city cars from Cleveland, Pittsburgh, Cincinnati and Shaker Heights.

Displays: Rare photos streetcar memorabilia and video tapes can be viewed in Ticket Office. The restored Baltimore & Ohio depot from Berea, Ohio, can also be seen.

Mark Brookins, Director

✔Gift Shop
✔Picnic Area

The Gerald E. Brookins Museum of
Electric Railways, Inc.
7100 Columbia Road
Olmsted Township, OH 44138
Phone (216) 235-4725

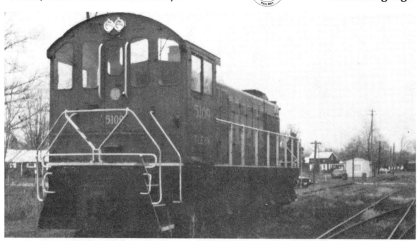

Location: Depots are located in Waterville at 49 North Sixth St. and in Grand Rapids at Third & Mill Sts. Both towns are southwest of Toledo on U.S. 24.

Ride: A 20-mile, 1½-hour round trip over a portion of the former Cloverleaf Division of the Nickel Plate Road. Train travels through villages, fields and woodlands and over a 900 ft. long bridge over the Maumee River and the old Miami & Erie Canal.

Schedule: Saturdays & Sundays, May 9-17 and September 12-November 1, lv. Waterville 12:30, 2:30 P.M. Lv. Grand Rapids 1:30, *3:30 P.M. Saturdays, Sundays & Holidays, May 23-September 7, lv. Waterville 12:30, 2:30, 4:30 P.M. Lv. Grand Rapids 1:30, 3:30, *5:30 P.M. Tuesdays & Thursdays, July 2-August 27, lv. Waterville 10:30 A.M., 1:30 P.M. Lv. Grand Rapids 11:30 A.M., *2:30 P.M.
(* One-way only) Subject to change without notice. Stopovers are permitted at each end of the line.

Fare: Adults $5.90, Seniors $5.30, Children $2.95.
One way fares, group rates available.

Locomotives: #5109, S-2 diesel, Alco (1948), ex-Chesapeake & Ohio.
#202, 0-6-0, Baldwin (1920), ex-Detroit Edison Co.
#1, 44-ton diesel, Whitcomb (1941), ex-Ann Arbor R.R.
#15, 0-6-0T, Porter (1908), ex-Brooklyn Eastern District Terminal.

Train: Cars on hand are used as required in the train. Including 1916 and 1924 New York Central coaches, 1930 Lackawanna electric commuter cars, Baltimore & Ohio coach, parlor car and Pullman car.

Displays: Cars not required in train. Also World War II troop sleeper, freight cars and maintenance of way equipment.

✔Gift Shop
✔Picnic Area
✔Memberships

 Toledo

Toledo, Lake Erie & Western Ry.
P.O. Box 168
Waterville, OH 43566
Phone (419) 878-1177 Waterville Depot
(419) 832-4671 Grand Rapids Depot

Location: Located in the Blue Mountains of Eastern Oregon. Take I-84 to Baker, then Highway 7 up the Powder River to Railroad Park in Sumpter Valley.

Ride: The SVR has 3½ miles of track in operation, with more under construction. A 7-mile round trip, with stops for wood and water, takes you through the dredge tailings left from the historic gold mining days. This is now a wild-life area with views of the rugged Elkhorn Mountains and beautiful Sumpter Valley.

Schedule: Saturdays, Sundays and Holidays, Memorial Day week-end thru last week-end in September. Train departs at 10:00 A.M., Noon, 2:00 & 4:00 P.M.

Fare: Adults $4.00, Children $3.00, under 6 free.
Family rate $10.00. Charters available.
Educational groups inquire for group reservations.

Locomotives: #3, 2-truck Heisler (1914), ex-W.H. Eccles Lumber Co. This engine is a 42-ton wood burner.

Train: Two excursion cars converted from ex-D.&R.G.W. flatcars. Original Sumpter Valley Railway caboose.

Displays: Former Sumpter Valley Railway 2-8-2's, #19 and #20 have been acquired from the White Pass & Yukon Route. These locomotives, built by Alco in 1920, are presently being restored for future service on the SVR. Also on the property is a former White Pass & Yukon rotary snow plow, cattle cars, a refrigerator car, steam pumps and a 125 horsepower stationary steam sawmill engine. Also the wood-splitting operation may be observed, visit the shops and walk the nature trails in the tailings.

✔Gift Shop
✔Picnic Area
✔Camping
✔Memberships

Sumpter Valley Railroad Restoration, Inc.
P.O. Box 389
Baker, OR 97814
Phone (503) 523-2410 Evenings

OREGON, COTTAGE GROVE
Oregon Pacific & Eastern Ry.

Steam, Diesel, scheduled
Standard gauge

Photo by Don Hunter

Location: The depot is located on the Village Green in Cottage Grove, 20 miles south of Eugene on Route I-5.

Ride: A 35-mile, 2-hour round trip through Oregon forest country. The train, known as "The Goose", follows the route of the Row River, past Dorena Lake to the foot of the Bohemia Mountains. At the end of the line, the train makes a loop and returns to Cottage Grove. The O.P.&E. R.R. is a common-carrier railroad serving local industries.

Schedule: Trains operate Saturdays and Sundays, May 23 through September 13. Steam trains leave at 10:00 A.M. and 2:00 P.M.
Charter trips available during the week.

Fare: Adults $7.50, Children (2-11) $3.75.
Reservations recommended.

Locomotives: #19, 2-8-2, Baldwin (1915), ex-McCloud River R.R.

Train: Air-conditioned train includes ex-Illinois Central coaches and lounge cars with beverage service.

M. F. Nikolaus, Vice-President Operations

✔Refreshments
✔Gift Shop

  Eugene

Oregon Pacific & Eastern Ry.
P.O. Box 565
Cottage Grove, OR 97424
Phone (503) 942-3368

Location: The Trolley Park, operated by the Oregon Electric Railway Histori-cal Society, is at Glenwood, 38 miles west of Portland on Route 6.

Ride: The Trolley Park is located at the far end of a valley. It is a specialized, old time picnic and camping park. To get there, you must ride the trolley from the end of the public road, past the shops and work area, into the forest. Overnight camping, swimming and fishing are a few of the experi-ences available at the Trolley Park.

Schedule: Week-ends and Holidays, May through October. Trolleys operate from 11:00 A.M. to 5:00 P.M.

Fare: Adults $3.00, Seniors & Students $2.00, Family Fare $7.50. Children under 5 free. Fare includes all facilities and unlimited trolley rides for the day.

Trolleys: #48, Blackpool, England double-deck tram (1904); #503 & #506, Portland semi-convertibles, Brill (1904); #1159, St. Louis/San Francisco P.C.C. car (1946); #1187, Sydney, Australia open car; #1304, British Columbia interurban (1911 rebuilt 1946).

Displays: Free museum exhibit, "How The Trolley Changed America". Also, a number of streetcars are on static display in the Shop and Car Barn.

🖊Gift Shop
🖊Picnic Area
🖊Camping
🖊Memberships

For information:
The Trolley Park
17744 S.W. Ivy Glenn Dr.
Beaverton, OR 97007
Phone (503) 642-5097 (Evenings)

Location: The Washington Park Zoo is located at 4001 S.W. Canyon Road in Portland.

Ride: The train takes passengers on a 4-mile round trip around the zoo and through forested hills to Washington Park. The route goes past the elephant enclosure giving passengers a close-up view of the zoo's world-famous pachyderm herd, another vantage point overlooks the new Alaska Tundra exhibit. The scenic ride includes a stop at Washington Park station with its panoramic view of Mount Hood, the City of Portland and Mount St. Helens. A gift shop at this end of the line features railroad memorabilia and souvenirs. Passengers may obtain a stopover pass at Washington Park station to visit the famous Rose Test Gardens and Japanese Garden, located nearby. Train patrons receive a 20% discount on admission to the Japanese Garden.

Schedule: Daily, mid-April through mid-October. Full 4-mile round trip operates Daily, Memorial Day through Labor Day, week-ends Spring and Fall. Shorter Zoo Loop trip operates week-days, Spring and Fall. Trains depart at frequent intervals.

Fare: Adults $1.75, Seniors & Children (3-11) $1.00, under 3 free.

Locomotives: #1, 4-4-0, oil-fired steam engine, replica of Virginia & Truckee's "Reno"; Zooliner, diesel replica of the General Motors "Aerotrain"; gas-powered "Orient Express"; gas-powered switcher and fire train.

Trains: Three passenger trains with streamlined cars and open coaches. Two work trains. Train is a registered Postal Railway Station.

✔Refreshments   Washington Park & Zoo Ry.
✔Gift Shop   4001 S.W. Canyon Road
✔Picnic Area   Portland, OR 97221
                                                Phone (503) 226-1561

 Portland

PENNSYLVANIA, ALTOONA
Railroaders Memorial Museum

Railway Museum
Standard gauge

Location: The Museum is located in the Station Mall Complex at 1300 Ninth Ave. The Conrail main-line is adjacent to the Museum.

Displays: The Exhibit Hall features artifacts and models dealing primarily with the Pennsylvania R.R. and the City of Altoona's huge P.R.R. shops and yards. The early development of the Pennsylvania R.R. is also covered. There is also an audio-visual presentation and an operating model railroad.

Rolling Stock: The display area features Pennsylvania R.R. GG-1 electric locomotive #4913, 0-4-0T switcher "Nancy", Vulcan (1918), ex-Berwind White Coal Co., the "Loretto", private railroad car of Charles M. Schwab, a dining car, 2 coaches, 3 sleeping cars, an express refrigerator car and other passenger equipment. Restoration of a solarium-sleeping car is in progress.

Schedule: Open Daily year-round (except closed Mondays, September thru May). Hours are 10:00 A.M. to 5:00 P.M., except Sundays, 12:30 P.M.

Admission: Adults $2.50, Seniors $1.75, Children $1.00, Family Rate $6.00.

Note: Pennsylvania R.R. K-4s steam locomotive, #1361, 4-6-2, Juniata Shops (1918), has been restored and is expected to begin excursion service during 1987. This engine was formerly displayed at the Horseshoe Curve.

History: The Altoona Locomotive Works of the Pennsylvania R.R. built 6783 steam locomotives for the railroad. The shops are now engaged in rebuilding diesel locomotives for Conrail. Located roughly halfway between Harrisburg and Pittsburgh, Altoona is on a busy Conrail main-line. The world-famous Horseshoe Curve is located 5½-miles west of Altoona.

Theodore J. Holland, Jr., Executive Director

✔Refreshments
✔Gift Shop
✔Memberships

Railroaders Memorial Museum
1300 Ninth Avenue
Altoona, PA 16603
Phone (814) 946-0834

 Altoona

142

Photo by George A. Forero, Jr.

Location: Located in a beautiful city park at 19th and Oak Streets.

Ride: Ride along the slopes of Pennsylvania coal mining country. The ride covers 1½ miles of outdoor coal mine trackage. Electric powered mine train provides an interesting tour of the inside of an anthracite mine last operated in 1931.

Schedule: Saturdays and Sundays, May, September and October. Daily operation Memorial Day through Labor Day. Train runs 10:00 A.M. to 5:30 P.M.; Mine Tour 10:00 A.M. to 6:00 P.M. Tunnel closes at 4:00 P.M. on the Saturday before Labor Day only.

Fare: Steam train: Adults $1.50, Children under 12, 75¢. Coal mine tour: Adults $3.50, Children under 12, $1.50.

Locomotives: "Henry Clay", 0-4-0T, Vulcan (1927), ex-Guadiano & Bros.

Train: Open mine cars with seats and a little red caboose.

Displays: A large community park adjoins the mine entrance. An extensive gift shop features unusual hard coal curios.

George C. Staudenmeir, Manager

✔Refreshments
✔Gift Shop
✔Picnic Area

Ashland Community Enterprises
Pioneer Tunnel Office, Dept. B
19th and Oak Street
Ashland, PA 17921
Phone (717) 875-3850

143

PENNSYLVANIA, BELLEFONTE
Bellefonte Historical R.R.

Diesel, scheduled
Standard gauge

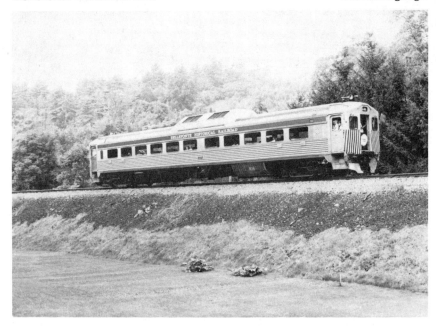

Photo by Mike Bezilla

Location: Bellefonte is located in the central part of Pennsylvania a short distance from Interstate 80. Trains travel over the lines of the Nittany & Bald Eagle R.R., formerly a branch of the Pennsylvania Railroad.

Ride: Regular runs make a 15-mile, 1-hour round trip through the scenic Bald Eagle Valley and include a stop at Curtin Village, a state-owned restored iron-mining site. Extra-fare Fall Foliage trips cover 60-miles in 3-hours.

Schedule: Budd Rail Diesel Car leaves Bellefonte Saturday and Sunday afternoons, Memorial Day week-end through the last week-end in September. Train leaves every 90 minutes. Fall Foliage trips operate Saturdays and Sundays in October. Other special trips include Christmas excursions, the week-end before Christmas.

Fare: Adults $3.00, Children $2.00, under 2 free.

Train: Rail Diesel Car (RDC) built by the Budd Co. in 1953. This car was built for the New Haven R.R. and numbered 41. Later sold to the Southeastern Pennsylvania Transportation Authority (SEPTA), it became No. 9167.

Displays: At the Bellefonte Train Station, a restored ex-P.R.R. structure built in 1888, is an operating N gauge layout of the Bellefonte-Curtin Village route. The station also contains historical photos and memorabilia of railroading in the area.

✔Refreshments
✔Gift Shop
✔Picnic Area
✔Memberships

Bellefonte Historical R.R.
The Train Station
Bellefonte, PA 16823
Phone (814) 355-0311

PENNSYLVANIA, GETTYSBURG
Gettysburg R.R.

Steam, scheduled
Standard gauge

Photo by George A. Forero, Jr.

Location: Depot is located off North Washington St. in historic Gettysburg.

Ride: The Gettysburg R.R. operates over a former Reading Co. branch line. Regular steam train makes a 16-mile, 1¼-hour round trip to Biglerville. Special runs on selected dates are made to Mt. Holly Springs, a 50-mile, 5-hour round trip.

Schedule: Gettysburg to Biglerville and return: Saturdays & Sundays, June thru October. Lv. 1:00 & 3:00 P.M. Daily operation, July & August, lvs. week-days 11:00 A.M. & 1:00 P.M. Steam or diesel power may be used during June and week-days in July & August.
To Mt. Holly Springs: Train lvs. 10:00 A.M. on July 11, August 8, September 12, October 3, 10, 11, 17. Reservations required.

Fare: To Biglerville: Adults $4.50, Children $3.00.
To Mt. Holly: Adults $12.00, Children $8.00.

Locomotives: #76, 2-8-0, Baldwin (1920), ex-Mississippian Ry.
#3254, 2-8-2, Canadian (1917), ex-Canadian National.

Train: Open side excursion cars, steel coaches, double-decker open car.

Special Events: Civil War Train Raid on September 19 at 1:00 & 3:00 P.M. Reservations not necessary.

✔Gift Shop

Gettysburg R.R.
P.O. Box 1267
Gettysburg, PA 17325
Phone (717) 334-6932

PENNSYLVANIA, JIM THORPE　　　　　　　　Steam, scheduled
Rail Tours, Inc.　　　　　　　　　　　　　　Standard gauge

Photo by George Harvan

Location: Trips run from the former Jersey Central R.R. station in the heart of Jim Thorpe. The site is on U.S. Route 209, 30 miles north of Allentown.

Ride: An 8-mile, 45-minute round trip from the station in Jim Thorpe to Nesquehoning over the Panther Valley R.R. The line was formerly a Jersey Central branch. During October trips are made to the end of the line at Haucks, a 34-mile, 2¾-hour round trip passing over the scenic Hometown trestle.

Schedule: Train runs Saturdays, Sundays & Holidays, May 23 to September 27. Train leaves hourly, 1:00 to 4:00 P.M. Fall Foliage trips to Haucks operate Saturdays, Sundays & Holidays in October. Lv. Jim Thorpe 1:30 P.M. (Also 10:00 A.M. certain days).

Fare: Regular Train: Adults $3.50, Children (5-11) $2.00, under 5 free.
Fall Foliage: Adults $10.00, Children (5-11) $6.00.

Locomotives: #972, 4-6-0, Montreal (1912), ex-Canadian Pacific Ry.

Train: Former Reading and Jersey Central open-window coaches, combines and open observation cars.

Displays: Museum, located in the historic Jim Thorpe (Mauch Chunk) railroad station, open Daily in summer, 11:00 A.M. to 4:30 P.M. Model train display nearby. The home of Asa Packer, founder of the Lehigh Valley R.R. is in town.

✔Gift Shop in depot

Rail Tours, Inc.
P.O. Box 285
Jim Thorpe, PA 18229
Phone (717) 325-3673
(717) 325-4606

146

Location: Depot is located at Kempton on Routes 143 or 737, a short distance north of Route I-78. The site is about 20 miles west of Allentown and 30 miles north of Reading, Pa.

Ride: A 6-mile, 40-minute round trip in the Pennsylvania Dutch section of the state. The train operates over a portion of the former Reading Company's Schuylkill & Lehigh branch. Steam-powered train is supplemented by a unique gasoline engined trolley car, the "Berksy".

Schedule: Steam train: Sundays & Holidays, May through October. Saturdays, Sundays & Holidays, June, July and August.
"Berksy" trolley operates Sundays in April, Saturdays in May, September and October. Trains leave hourly, 1:00 to 4:00 P.M., Sundays to 5:00 P.M.

Fare: Adults $2.50, Children $1.25, tax included. Train ticket entitles passengers to unlimited rides during day purchased.

Locomotives: #2, 0-4-0T, Porter (1920), ex-Colorado Fuel & Iron.
#65, 0-6-0T, Porter (1930), ex-Safe Harbor Water & Power.
#35, gas-electric switcher, Mack/S.W.M.R.R. Co. (1927).
#20, gas-mechanical switcher, Whitcomb (1935).

Train: Coaches, combine, open gondola, caboose.

Displays: Operating HO model layout (Steam Sundays). Special cars available for group charter on days when steam train operates. Two old passenger stations, restored bobber caboose. Picnic groves at depot and along the right-of-way.

✔Refreshments   Wanamaker, Kempton & Southern, Inc.
✔Gift Shop   Box 24
✔Picnic Area   Kempton, PA 19529
✔Antique Shop   Phone (215) 756-6469
                                   (215) 437-1239

Location: The West Shore R.R. is located in the central part of the state, in Union County at Mifflinburg. Passengers board trains at the new station in Mifflinburg.

Ride: Two rides of differing lengths are offered. A 9-mile, 1-hour round-trip to Vicksburg and an 18-mile, 2-hour round-trip to Lewisburg. This line was once a branch of the Pennsylvania R.R.

Schedule: Trains operate May 23-June 21: Saturdays 11 A.M. & 1:30 P.M., Sundays 2 P.M.; June 23-Sept. 6: Wed. & Sat. 11 A.M. & 1:30 P.M., Tues., Thurs. & Sun. 2 P.M.; Sept. 9-30: Wed. & Sat. 11 A.M. & 1:30 P.M., Sun. 2 P.M.; Oct. 4-25: Sundays 2 P.M.; Dec. 6-20: Sundays 2 & 3 P.M. No trains Labor Day.

Fare: Adults $5.00 or $3.00, Children $2.00 or $1.50.

Locomotives: #8525, SW-1 diesel, E.M.D. (1950), ex-Pennsylvania R.R.

Train: Steel coaches from Pennsylvania, Jersey Central, Erie and Lackawanna railroads.

Displays: #2233, GP-30 diesel, E.M.D. (1963), ex-P.R.R. Painted in Pennsylvania R.R. colors.

✔Refreshments
✔Gift Shop

West Shore Rail Excursions
196 N. 3rd Street
Mifflinburg, PA 17844
Phone (717) 966-9390

PENNSYLVANIA, NEW HOPE
New Hope Steam Railway & Museum

**Steam, scheduled
Standard gauge**

Location: Trains depart from depots located at Bridge St. (Rt. 179) in New Hope, and on Rt. 413 in Buckingham, both in Bucks County.

Ride: A 14-mile, 1½-hour round trip between New Hope and Buckingham, climbing mountain grades and passing through rock cuts and over trestles, including the famed curved trestle featured in the "Perils of Pauline" serials of long ago.

Schedule: Train operates Saturdays, Sundays & Holidays, May through October.

Lv. New Hope *11:30 A.M.	Lv. Buckingham *12:30 P.M.
1:30 P.M.	2:30 P.M.
3:30 P.M.	4:30 P.M.

(*Sundays only) (Holidays are Memorial Day, July 4, Labor Day)

Fare: Adults $5.00, Children $3.00.

Locomotives: #40, 2-8-0, Baldwin (1925), ex-Cliffside R.R.
#9, 0-6-0, Alco (1942), ex-Virginia Blue Ridge Ry.
#739, SW-1 diesel, E.M.D., ex-Pennsylvania R.R.
#302, Baldwin diesel, ex-Pennsylvania R.R.

Special Events: Railfan Week-end, last week-end in October. Santa Claus Specials in December (reservations required). Charter trips available.

Train: 1930 vintage Reading steel open-window coaches and caboose.

Displays: #1533, 4-6-0, Montreal (1911), ex-Canadian National Rys.; Bangor & Aroostook baggage car; Jersey Central R.P.O. car and various other railroad equipment.

C. N. Vallette, V.P. Operations

✓Gift Shop
✓Free Parking at Buckingham

Mailing Address:
New Hope Steam Railway & Museum
P.O. Box 612
Huntingdon Valley, PA 19006
Phone (215) 862-2707

PENNSYLVANIA, NORTH EAST
Lake Shore Railway Historical Society, Inc.

Railway Museum
Standard gauge

Photo by Vincent Moskalczyk

Location: The Museum is the former New York Central passenger station at Wall & Robinson Sts. in North East. About 15 miles east of Erie, Pa., the site is handy to Routes I-90 and U.S. 20.

Displays: The station was built by the Lake Shore & Michigan Southern Ry. in 1899. There are extensive displays of railroadiana inside the restored structure, including one of the two locomotive display models built by Heisler in 1915. Additional displays are contained in three World War II troop sleepers and a former Pittsburg & Shawmut wood caboose. Other items on display include a wooden B.&L.E. boxcar, three generations of refrigerator cars, a Whitcomb switcher and a fireless Heisler locomotive. Passenger equipment on the display sidings include light and heavyweight sleepers, baggage cars, an operating diner, a dome car and an L.S.&M.S. 1890 wooden business car. The museum is located adjacent to Conrail (NYC) and Norfolk & Western (NKP) mainlines.

Schedule: Visitors are welcome Saturdays, Sundays & Holidays, May 16 through September 27. During June, July & August, Museum is also open Wednesdays, Thursdays & Fridays. Museum hours are 1:00 to 5:00 P.M.

Admission: No admission charge.

Excursions: A variety of rail excursions are planned for 1987. Write for information.

✔Refreshments
✔Gift Shop
✔Memberships

Lake Shore Railway Historical Society, Inc.
P.O. Box 571
North East, PA 16428
Phone (814) 825-2724

 Erie

150

Photo by John J. Hilton

Location: Located in central Pennsylvania at Rockhill Furnace adjacent to Orbisonia on Route 522. Use Fort Littleton or Willow Hill exits of Pennsylvania Turnpike.

Ride: The East Broad Top R.R., chartered in 1856, was the last operating narrow-gauge railroad east of the Mississippi. The road hauled coal, freight, mail, express and passengers for more than 80 years. Today the East Broad Top still transports passengers through the beautiful Aughwick Valley with its own preserved locomotives. Trains run from the historic depot at Rockhill Furnace to the picnic grove, where the train is turned. Returning, the train is once again turned for the next trip. The 10-mile ride takes 45 minutes. The railroad is a Registered National Historic Landmark.

Schedule: Saturdays and Sundays, June, September and October. Daily during July and August. Trains leave hourly from 11:00 A.M. to 4:00 P.M.

Fare: Adults $5.00, Children $2.50, under 5 free.

Locomotives: #12, 2-8-2, Baldwin (1911)   #14, 2-8-2, Baldwin (1912)
#15, 2-8-2, Baldwin (1914)   #17, 2-8-2, Baldwin (1918)
All built for East Broad Top R.R.

Train: Wooden coaches, parlor cars, open cars.

Displays: Large railroad yard with shop buildings, operating roundhouse and turntable. E.B.T. freight cars, cabooses, work equipment and gas-electric car can be seen.

✔Gift Shop
✔Picnic Area
✔Memberships
✔Camping Area

East Broad Top R.R.
Rockhill Furnace, PA 17249
Phone (814) 447-3011

PENNSYLVANIA, ORBISONIA
Shade Gap Electric Ry.

Electric, scheduled
Standard gauge

Photo by Salomon Bros.

Location: Trolley passengers board cars at platform across the street from the East Broad Top R.R. station in Rockhill Furnace, PA.

Ride: Trolleys operate over dual-gauge trackage on the former Shade Gap branch of the East Broad Top R.R for a 2-mile, 20-minute trip. Standard gauge trolleys meet narrow-gauge steam trains.

Schedule: Week-ends and Holidays, May 23 through November 1, 1987. Cars depart half-hourly, 11:30 A.M. to 4:30 P.M. and are scheduled to meet steam trains. 1987 is our 25th Anniversary, call or write for special events (enclose SASE).

Fare: All day ticket, $1.50 per person. Family rate $5.00.
Group and charter rates available. See Discount Coupon in this book.

Trolleys: #172, "Toonerville" type, Porto, Portugal (1929);
#249, double-truck Brill semi-convertible (1905);
#311, double-truck Birney (1923), Johnstown, PA;
#315, Chicago, Aurora & Elgin interurban , Kuhlman (1909);
#1875, summer car, St. Louis (1912), Rio de Janeiro;
Liberty Liner "Independence Hall", (former North Shore Electroliner #803-804) operates by arrangement.

Displays: 1898 snowsweeper; Washington, D.C. PCC car; 1910 snow-sweeper from Scranton, PA; 1930 drop-side work car; York Street Railways #163 currently under restoration. Shop and car barn tours available. Artifact and photo display in museum. Other cars in storage.

Steve Kistler, Head of Operations

✔Refreshments
✔Gift Shop
✔Picnic Area
✔Memberships

Railways to Yesterday, Inc.
P.O. Box 1601
Allentown, PA 18105
Phone (814) 447-9576 (in season)
(717) 367-6754 or
(215) 434-0624 (other times)

Courtesy of the Franklin Institute

Location: The Franklin Institute is located at 20th and the Parkway in the City of Philadelphia.

Displays: This famous museum features an extensive transportation display. Locomotives on exhibit range from the "Rocket" which was built in England in 1838, a Reading R.R. 4-4-0 in service until 1883 and Baldwin No. 60000. This huge engine, a 4-10-2 type, is 101 ft. long and weighs 350 tons. It is a 3-cylinder compound engine with a water tube firebox, was constructed in 1926 and bears the builder's number 60,000 of the Baldwin Locomotive Works. This giant engine moves back and forth about 10 feet at regular intervals, powered by an electric motor.

Admission: Adults $4.50, Seniors $3.00, Children (4-12) $3.50, under 4 free.

Schedule: Daily, year-round, 10:00 A.M. to 5:00 P.M. Sundays, Noon to 5:00 P.M. Closed New Year's Day, Memorial Day, July 4, Labor Day, Thanksgiving Day, December 24 & 25.

Note: The Franklin Institute Science Museum features displays and exhibits in the fields of aviation, astronomy, light, printing and maritime history, among others. The Museum is a well-known landmark in the City of Philadelphia.
Joel N. Bloom, President

✔Gift Shop
✔Restaurant
✔Memberships

The Franklin Institute
20th & The Parkway
Philadelphia, PA 19103
Phone (215) 448-1000

 Philadelphia

PENNSYLVANIA, PHILADELPHIA
Penn's Landing Trolley

Electric, scheduled
Standard gauge

Photo by Richard C. Roden

Location: The Penn's Landing Trolley operates along Philadelphia's historic waterfront. Cars are boarded at Delaware Ave. and Dock St., or Delaware Ave. and Spruce St.

Ride: A 2.2-mile, 20-minute round trip along the Delaware River waterfront over trackage of the Philadelphia Belt Line R.R. Cars pass the Port of History Museum and the City's fleet of historic ships. These include the sailing ships "Gazela Primeiro" and the "Moshulu", the submarine "Becuna" and the historic cruiser U.S.S. Olympia.

Schedule: Saturdays, Sundays & Holidays, April 19 through December 6. Also Thursdays & Fridays from June 18 to Labor Day. Cars operate every 30 minutes or less from 11:00 A.M. to dusk. Santa Claus Specials operate December 12-13, 1987.

Fare: Tickets are purchased at the Spruce St. ticket booth of the cruiser Olympia. Tickets also available on board cars. All-day Pass, Adults $1.50, Children under 12, 50¢.

Trolleys: #26, double-truck "Hog Island" car, Brill (1918), ex-Philadelphia Suburban Transit, ex-Phila. Rapid Transit.
#80, Brill Master Unit (1931), ex-Philadelphia Suburban Transit.
#76, double-truck, center-entrance interurban car, Brill (1926) ex-Phila. Suburban Transit.

Note: The Penn's Landing Trolley is operated by the Buckingham Valley Trolley Assn. The group has preserved a number of trolleys and interurban cars from the Philadelphia area.

✔Memberships

 Philadelphia

Penn's Landing Trolley
P.O. Box 7285
Philadelphia, PA 19101
Phone (215) 627-0807

154

Photo by John E. Helbok

Location: Trains depart from the former D.L.&W. depot in Scranton, now the Hilton at Lackawanna Station Hotel. Take Exit 53 of I-380. Passengers may also board at Pocono Summit, PA, 32 miles south of Scranton, just off I-380.

Ride: Steamtown has extended its trips over the former Lackawanna mainline and now offers a choice of three train rides. A 26-mile round trip, Scranton - Moscow; a 64-mile round trip, Scranton - Pocono Summit; or a 38-mile round trip, Pocono Summit - Moscow.

Schedule: May 2 - June 14 and Sept. 12-20, Week-ends & Holidays only, lv. Scranton 10:15 A.M. & 12:55 P.M. Lv. Pocono Summit 10:10 A.M. & 12:30 P.M.
June 20 - Sept. 7, Daily operation. Lv. Scranton 10:15 A.M., 12:55 & 3:10 P.M. Lv. Pocono Summit 10:10 A.M., 12:30 & 3:10 P.M.
Sept. 26 - Nov. 1, Daily operation. Lv. Scranton 10:15 A.M., 12:55 P.M. & *3:10 P.M. Lv. Pocono Summit 10:10 A.M., 12:30 P.M. & *3:10 P.M. (*Week-ends only).

Fare: Scranton-Moscow: Adults $8.50, Children (under 12) $5.50.
Pocono Summit-Moscow: Adults $14.95, Children (under 12) $10.95.
Scranton-Pocono Summit, either direction, Adults $19.95, Children (under 12) $14.95.

Locomotives: #2317, 4-6-2, Montreal (1923), ex-Canadian Pacific Ry.
FP-7 diesel, EMD (1952), ex-MILW #97C.
#1293, 4-6-2, Canadian (1948), ex-Canadian Pacific Ry.

Displays: A sample of the world-famous Steamtown collection is on display at the Scranton station. Locomotives include Union Pacific "Big Boy" #4012, Boston & Maine #3713 and Rahway Valley #15.
In the Fall of 1986, legislation was passed putting the Steamtown Collection and the former Delaware, Lackawanna & Western R.R. facilities in Scranton under the auspices of the National Park Service for future development.

✔Refreshments
✔Gift Shop
✔Picnic Area

Steamtown, U.S.A.
P.O. Box F
Scranton, PA 18501
Phone (in PA) (800) 622-RAIL
(other) (800) 533-RAIL

Photo by Raymond L. McFadden

Location: Stewartstown is located south of York, a few miles from the Maryland border. It is 4 miles east of I-83 on Pa. Route 851. Trains leave from station at Hill and Pennsylvania Ave.

Ride: A 15-mile, 1¾-hour round trip between Stewartstown and New Freedom, Pa. on Lincoln's route to Gettysburg. These rural excursions operate on a railroad which was opened a century ago.

Schedule: Trains operate Sundays & Holidays, May 10 through September 27. Trains leave at 1:30 and 3:30 P.M. Fall Foliage Specials operate Saturdays & Sundays, October 3 thru November 8, go from Stewartstown to Shrewsbury. Lv. Saturdays at 12:30 and 2:30 P.M., Sundays at 11:00 A.M., 1:00 and 3:00 P.M.

Fare: All trips: Adults $5.00, Children (6-11) $3.00, under 6 free.

Locomotives: #9, 35-ton Plymouth ML-8, Plymouth (1943), Stewartstown R.R.
#10, 44-ton diesel, G.E. (1946), ex-Coudersport & Port Allegany.

Train: Former Reading Company all-steel, open-window day coaches.

Displays: Station depot, waiting room and ticket window virtually unchanged since its 1915 appearance.

Note: All ticket sales limited to capacity of train and sold on first-come, first-served basis.

Stewartstown Railroad
P.O. Box 155
Stewartstown, PA 17363
Phone (717) 993-2936

The Railroad Museum of Pennsylvania

Location: The Museum is located on Penna. Route 741, opposite the Strasburg Rail Road.

Displays: The Railroad Museum of Pennsylvania houses one of the world's finest collections of steam, electric and diesel-electric locomotives, passenger cars and related memorabilia. The large museum building covers 4 tracks which exhibit many locomotives and passenger cars, some made up into complete period trains. From the second floor exhibit area, a catwalk overlooks the trains below. Outside, in the museum's extensive yard (open select week-ends) are over 40 locomotives and cars.

Schedule: Museum is open year-round. Open Daily, 9:00 A.M. to 5:00 P.M. except Sundays from Noon to 5:00 P.M. Closed on Mondays only from November through April. Museum will also be closed on certain holidays.

Admission: Adults $2.00, Seniors $1.50, Children (6-11) $1.00, under 6 free.

Locomotives: A few of the engines indoors include: "Tahoe", 2-6-0, Baldwin (1875); Pennsylvania R.R. #1187, 2-8-0, Juniata (1888); P.R.R. #5741, 4-6-0, Juniata (1924); P.R.R. GG-1 Electric #4935.
Outdoors are P.R.R. K-4s #3750, 4-6-2, Juniata (1920); L-1a #520, 2-8-2, Baldwin (1916); M-1b #6755, 4-8-2, Juniata (1930) and many others.

Rolling Stock: A sample of the cars on display include Cumberland Valley wooden combine (1855), P.R.R. combine #4639 (1895) and other early P.R.R. express, baggage, mail and passenger coaches. Also Pullman car "Lotos Club", Western Maryland Ry. business car #203 and other passenger equipment.

Robert L. Emerson, Director

Railroad Museum of Pennsylvania
P.O. Box 15
Strasburg, PA 17579
Phone (717) 687-8628

 Lancaster

Photo by Howard Pincus

Location: Strasburg Rail Road is located on Route 741 in the Pennsylvania Dutch country a short distance from Lancaster, Pa.

Ride: A 9-mile, 45-minute round trip from Strasburg to Paradise. Train travels through lush farm lands, turns around adjacent to the electrified main line of Amtrak and Conrail.

Schedule: Week-ends, mid-March through mid-December. Daily, May through October. Number of trips per day varies with the season from 4 to 14. During July and August 2 trains operate providing half-hourly service. Complete timetables sent upon request.

Fare: Adults $4.50, Children $2.50.

Locomotives: #31, 0-6-0, Baldwin (1908), ex-Canadian National.
#89, 2-6-0, Canadian (1910), ex-Canadian National.
#90, 2-10-0, Baldwin (1924), ex-Great Western Ry.
#1223, 4-4-0, Juniata (1906), #7002, 4-4-2, Juniata (1902), both leased from Railroad Museum of Pennsylvania.

Train: Open platform wooden combine and coaches. "Hello Dolly" open observation cars.

Displays: Strasburg R.R. is one of the oldest and busiest of the steam tourist railroads in the country. A large collection of historic cars and locomotives is on display. The Railroad Museum of Pennsylvania, adjacent to Strasburg, displays an extensive collection of railroad equipment.

✔Refreshments
✔Gift Shop
✔Picnic Area
✔Restaurant

Strasburg Rail Road
P.O. Box 96
Strasburg, PA 17579
Phone (717) 687-7522

Lancaster

Location: The museum is located on Paradise Lane, a short distance from the Strasburg R.R. and the Railroad Museum of Pennsylvania.

Displays: The Toy Train Museum is operated by the Train Collectors Association, a non-profit organization founded in 1954. Trains on display range in age from before the turn of the century to the present time. There are cast iron trains, tinplate trains and modern plastic trains. Trains that Dad and Grandad played with are tastefully displayed. There are also three operating toy train layouts complete with villages and an old time movie is shown.

Schedule: Open week-ends in April, November and first 2 week-ends in December. Open Daily, May 1 through October 31. Also open Good Friday, Easter Monday, Thanksgiving Friday and Christmas Week (weather permitting). Hours are 10:00 A.M. to 5:00 P.M.

Admission: Adults $2.25, Seniors $2.00, Children (7-12) 75¢.

Note: The Train Collectors Association was founded in 1954 to bring together persons interested in toy trains, publish periodicals and other literature, establish collecting standards, and to share information with others. For membership information, write to the National Business Office at the address shown.

✔Memberships

 Lancaster

Toy Train Museum
P.O. Box 248
Strasburg, PA 17579
Phone (717) 687-8976

Photo by Carl Price

Location: The Blue Mountain & Reading R.R. is located at Temple, 2 miles north of Reading on Route 61. Trains leave from depot on Tuckerton Rd., between Routes 61 and 222.

Ride: A 26-mile, 1½-hour round trip from Temple to Hamburg and return. Train runs along the historic Schuylkill Canal and Schuylkill River on 50 mph trackage. This is steam power the way it used to be. Train may also be boarded at Hamburg station.

Schedule: Train operates Daily, Memorial Day through Labor Day.
Lvs. Temple 11:00 A.M., 1:00 & 3:00 P.M. Steam-power Wednesday thru Sunday, diesel power Monday & Tuesday. Also runs Fridays, Saturdays & Sundays during April, May, September, October & November. Write for complete timetables.

Fare: Adults $6.00, Seniors $5.00, Children (3-12) $4.00, under 3 free.

Locomotives: #425, 4-6-2, Baldwin (1928), ex-Gulf, Mobile & Ohio R.R.
#2102, 4-8-4, Reading Shops (1945), ex-Reading Ry. Co.
#5706 & #5898, E-8A diesels, E.M.D. (1952), ex-P.R.R.
#600 & #601, CF-7 diesels, ex-Santa Fe.
#9166, 9168, 9169, R.D.C. cars, Budd Co. (1958), ex-SEPTA.

Train: Completely restored Delaware, Lackawanna & Western R.R. coaches with lights and electric heat.

Displays: Former Canadian Pacific Ry. "Royal Hudson" #2839 is on display.
Therman Madeira, Passenger Agent

✔Refreshments
✔Gift Shop
✔Picnic Area

Blue Mountain & Reading R.R.
P.O. Box 425
Hamburg, PA 19526
Phone (215) 562-4083

PENNSYLVANIA, TITUSVILLE
Oil Creek & Titusville R.R.

Diesel, scheduled
Standard gauge

Location: The historic oil region of Pennsylvania is located in the northwestern part of the state, easily accessible from Interstates 79 and 80. Trains depart from Perry St. Station, on South Perry St. in Titusville and Rynd Farm, 3½-miles north of Oil City on Route 8.

Ride: A 27-mile, 2½-hour round trip through the Oil Creek valley, birthplace of the oil industry. The former Pennsylvania R.R. line passes through Oil Creek State Park and passengers may stop at Petroleum Centre and Drake Well Park.

Schedule: Train runs Saturdays, Sundays and Holidays, May 1 through November 1. Also runs Fridays, June 19 through August 28 and during October. Trains leave Titusville 11:40 A.M. & 3:10 P.M., leave Rynd Farm 1:30 & *5:00 P.M. (* One-way).

Fare: Adults $7.00, Seniors $6.00, Children (3-12) $4.00.
One-way fares available. Group rates available.
Tickets may be ordered by mail, write for information.

Locomotives: #75, S-2 diesel, Alco (1947), ex-South Buffalo Ry.

Train: Open-window coaches from Delaware, Lackawanna & Western, Wabash Cannon Ball coach #1399 and Pullman heavyweight 6-double bedroom, 6-section sleeping car "Poplar Trail".

Note: Oil Creek State Park has picnic facilities, bicycle rental, hiking trails and a bike trail on the original right-of-way of the Oil Creek R.R. (circa 1860). Drake Well Park has a working, steam-operated replica of the world's first oil well, plus the Drake Well Museum.
The railroad is sponsored by the Oil Creek Railway Historical Society.

✔Refreshments
✔Gift Shop
✔Picnic Area

Oil Creek & Titusville R.R.
P.O. Box 68
Oil City, PA 16301
Phone (814) 676-1733

Location: Arden Trolley Museum is located 2 miles from downtown Washington, Pa. on North Main Street Extension. The site is on the former broad-gauge main line of the Pittsburgh-Washington interurban.

Ride: A 1-mile, 20-minute ride over a section of the former Washington interurban line of the Pittsburgh Railways.

Schedule: Saturdays, Sundays & Holidays, May through September. Daily, July 4 through Labor Day. Cars operate from Noon to 5:00 P.M. Eighth Annual Trolley Fair will be held on Sunday, June 28, 1987. Includes Trolley Carbarn Theater, demonstrations, arts and crafts. Gandy Dancer contest and outside model railroad display.

Fare: Adults $2.00 (all-day pass), Children $1.00, under 5 free.
Group rates available by advance reservation.

Trolleys: #3756, double-truck steel car from Pittsburgh Rys.; #5326, double-truck steel car from Philadelphia Rapid Transit; #832, double-truck steel car from New Orleans Public Service Co.; #66, double-truck, center-door car from Philadelphia Suburban Transit. Three more cars have been acquired from Philadelphia.

Displays: Two dozen interesting cars are on exhibit ranging from early wooden types to two P.C.C. cars from Pittsburgh Rys. There is a collection of standard gauge railroad equipment. Locomotives include #69, 0-6-0T, Baldwin (1930), ex-Duquesne Slag Products, a rare 1930 diesel-electric engine and a Baldwin-Westinghouse electric loco. A Bessemer & Lake Erie combine, 2 cabooses and freight cars complete the display.

✔Refreshments
✔Gift Shop
✔Picnic Area
✔Memberships

Pennsylvania Railway Museum Assn.
P.O. Box 832
Pittsburgh, PA 15230
Phone (412) 734-5780

Location: In the western part of South Dakota, near Mt. Rushmore National Monument, the Black Hills Central's 1880 Train is one of the country's oldest tourist-type steam railroads. This year marks the 31st year of operation of the Black Hills Central R.R. The scenic line runs between Hill City and Keystone over railroad once a part of the Burlington Route.

Ride: An 18-mile, 2-hour round trip between Hill City and Keystone Junction. The train travels through forests and mountains near Mt. Rushmore National Monument. The ruling grade on the line is 4%.

Schedule: Train operates from mid-June through late August (until Labor Day if weather permits). Steam train operates Daily. Lv. Hill City at 8:15 & 10:30 A.M. and 1:00 & 3:15 P.M. Lv. Keystone at 9:00 & 11:30 A.M. and 2:00 & *4:00 P.M. (*One-way). Note: There are no morning trains on Sundays and no 8:15/9:00 A.M. trains on Fridays or Saturdays.

Fare: Adults $12.00, Children $8.00, under 6 free.

Locomotives: #7, 2-6-2, Baldwin (1919), ex-Prescott & Northwestern R.R. #104, 2-6-2T, Baldwin (1926), ex-Peninsula Terminal R.R.

Train: Vintage open-platform wooden coaches, half-open coaches and open observation cars.

Displays: #103, 2-6-2T, Baldwin (1922), ex-Peninsula Terminal R.R. #14, 2-8-0, Baldwin (1914), ex-Duluth & Northeastern R.R. Narrow-gauge engines and cars and modern streamlined Zephyr equipment.

Note: Locomotive #7 and some of its cars have appeared in episodes of "Gunsmoke", the Disney film "Scandalous John" and the made-for-TV movie "Orphan Train".

✔Refreshments
✔Gift Shop
✔Picnic Area
✔Free Parking

Black Hills Central R.R.
Box 1880
Hill City, SD 57745
Phone (605) 574-2222

TENNESSEE, CHATTANOOGA
Tennessee Valley Railroad Museum

Steam, scheduled
Standard gauge

Location: 4119 Cromwell Road near Jersey Pike Exit of Tenn. Hwy. 153, only 1½-miles west of the I-75 interchange with Hwy. 153.

Ride: A 6-mile, 45-minute round trip, much on original E.T.V.&G. roadbed, across Chickamauga Creek, SBD system railroad, Tunnel Boulevard and across 986 ft. long Missionary Ridge Tunnel to East Chattanooga Depot, where shop, turntable and displays are located. Train is turned on wye at Grand Junction (Cromwell Rd.), where depot features gift shop, displays, slide-show, restrooms and Depot Delicatessen.

Schedule: Open Saturdays & Sundays, April thru November. Open Daily, June 8 thru September 6. Steam-powered trains depart East Chattanooga 40 min. past the hour, Grand Junction 5 min. past the hour from 10:30 A.M. to 4:30 P.M., except opens at 12:30 P.M. on Sundays.

"Downtown Arrow" service to downtown Chattanooga and Freight Depot Marketplace. Consult Agent for schedule. Fare: Adults $10.00, Children $7.00.

Fare: Museum train: Adults $5.50, Children $3.00, under 6 free.

Locomotives: #610, 2-8-0, Baldwin (1952), ex-U.S. Army (Operating)
#630, 2-8-0, Alco (1904), ex-Southern Ry. (Operating)
#3, 0-4-0T, Alco (1928), ex-Southern Wood Products (Operating)
#8669, 8677, 8014, RSD-1 diesels, Alco (1941-44), ex-U.S. Army
#722, 2-8-0, Baldwin (1904), ex-Southern Ry.
#6910, 2-8-2, Baldwin (1920), ex-Southern Ry.
#349, 4-4-0, Baldwin (1891), ex-Central of Georgia.
#509, 4-6-0, Baldwin (1910), ex-Louisiana & Arkansas.
ACT-1, Dept. of Trans. Experimental Electric Train.

Train: Heavyweight coaches with adjustable windows, air-conditioned lightweight coach Central of Georgia #907, Diner #158.

Displays: "Discovery Trail" has walking tour of caboose, T.C. Office Car 102, display car, theater car, diner, Pullmans, ACT-1 train. See Tennessee's only steam locomotive repair shop in action.

Robert M. Soule, President; D. K. Marshall, Operations Manager

✔Refreshments
✔Gift Shop
✔Memberships

Tennessee Valley Railroad Museum
4119 Cromwell Road
Chattanooga, TN 37421
Phone (615) 894-8028

TENNESSEE, JACKSON
Casey Jones Home R.R. Museum

Railway Museum
Standard gauge

Location: Jackson is located in western Tennessee on Interstate 40. The Museum is at the Highway 45 By-Pass exit of I-40.

Displays: The restored home of legendary railroad hero Casey Jones is now open to the public in its new location. This is the original home in which Casey Jones, his wife Janie, and their three children were living at the time of his death on April 3, 1900. The Museum includes personal items used by Casey Jones as well as numerous railroad artifacts and memorabilia.

Schedule: Open Daily year-round. Summer hours 9:00 A.M. to 5:00 P.M. Winter hours 10:00 A.M. to 5:00 P.M. Closed on Easter, Thanksgiving and Christmas.

Admission: Adults $3.00, Children (6-12) $1.75, under 6 free. Group rates available for parties of 20 or more.

Locomotives: #382, 4-6-0, Baldwin (1905), ex-Clinchfield #99. This engine is similar to the ten-wheeler in which Casey Jones made his famous last ride.

Train: Two circa 1890 coaches plus a modern G.M.&O. caboose which serves as a unique sign at the entrance.

Other: Also located in Casey Jones Village is Brooks Shaws' Old Country Store, a restaurant, gift shop and the Carl Perkins Music Museum.

J. Lawrence Taylor, Executive Vice-President

✔Refreshments
✔Gift Shop
✔Picnic Area
✔Restaurant
✔Memberships
✔Lifetime Pass

Casey Jones Home Railroad Museum
Jackson, TN 38305
Phone (901) 668-1223

TEXAS, CORPUS CHRISTI-LAREDO
Texas Mexican Railway Co.

Diesel, scheduled
Standard gauge

Location: The "Tex-Mex Express" operates between Corpus Christi and Laredo in south Texas. The train runs over the main-line of the Texas Mexican R.R. Passenger trains leave from 111 N. Alameda in Corpus Christi and from 1203 Monctezuma in Laredo.

Ride: A 320-mile, 11-hour round trip from Corpus Christi to Laredo and return, including a 2-hour stopover in Laredo. Passengers may travel one-way if desired. Train also serves stations enroute. Train travels through the farm and ranch lands of south Texas.

Schedule: Fridays, Saturdays & Sundays, year-round. Train departs Corpus Christi 9:30 A.M., returns 8:30 P.M.

Fare: Full round-trip: Adults $39.95, Children, 12 and under, half-fare. For reservations, call phone numbers shown below. Tickets may be purchased at depots in Corpus Christi or Laredo.

Locomotives: Model GP-38-2 E.M.D. diesels.

Train: Five restored and air-conditioned cars, including four coaches and a lounge car. Lounge car features a snack-bar and a full-service bar.

<table>
<tr><td>

✔Refreshments on train
✔Gift Shop on train
✔Free Parking

</td><td>

Texas Mexican Railway Co.
P.O. Box 419
Laredo, TX 78042
Phone (512) 722-6411
(800) 331-3182 (In Texas)

</td></tr>
</table>

TEXAS, DALLAS
Age of Steam Railroad Museum

Railway Museum
Standard gauge

Photo by Ken Walters

Location: The Museum is located 2 miles east of downtown Dallas on Washington St. The site is on the north side of the grounds of the State Fair of Texas at Fair Park. From I-30 eastbound, take Exit 47A to Parry Ave. then left 3 blocks to the entrance. From I-30 westbound, use Exit 47A to the right onto Exposition Ave., then left on Parry Ave.

Displays: A nostalgic journey back to the days of steam locomotives and name passenger trains. Operated by the Southwest Railroad Historical Society, the museum features some of the world's largest steam, diesel-electric & electric locomotives. There is a superlative collection of heavyweight passenger equipment including the M-K-T dining car "George S. Denison", the Fort Worth & Denver business car "Texland" and the newly-restored Santa Fe Parlor-Club car No. 3231. There are also various chair and Pullman cars, vintage freight cars and cabooses, as well as Dallas's oldest train station and numerous railroad artifacts. Come blow the steam locomotive whistles and enjoy one of the nation's foremost railroad collections.

Schedule: Open Saturdays & Sundays, year-round, 11:00 A.M. to 5:00 P.M. Also Thursdays & Fridays, 9:00 A.M. to 1:00 P.M. Open Daily during the State Fair of Texas in October. Group tours available by appointment.

Admission: Adults $2.00, Children (16 and under) $1.00.

Locomotives: #4018, 4-8-8-4, Alco (1942), Union Pacific "Big Boy".
#1625, 2-10-0, Alco (1918), Eagle-Picher Mining Co.
#4501, 4-8-4, Baldwin (1942), Frisco Lines.
#7, 0-6-0, Baldwin (1923), Union Terminal Co. (Dallas).
#6913, DDA40X, E.M.D., Union Pacific "Centennial".
#4906, GG-1 Electric, Amtrak, (ex-P.R.R. #4903).
M-160, Diesel-electric "Doodlebug", Santa Fe.

✔Refreshments in park
✔Gift Shop
✔Memberships

Amtrak ➤ Dallas

Southwest Railroad Historical Society
P.O. Box 26369
Dallas, TX 75226-0369
Phone (214) 421-8754
(214) 522-1025

Displays: The Museum is located on 5 acres surrounding the old Santa Fe Union Station. Galveston was served by the passenger trains of the Santa Fe, Rock Island, Burlington and Katy. The largest rail collection in the Southwest is located here, including steam and diesel locomotives, passenger and freight cars. Spectacular sound and light shows present the history and development of Galveston. The People's Gallery returns to "A Moment Frozen in Time" where ghosts of travelers past await boarding calls in the restored 1930's art deco depot. A working HO gauge model of the Port of Galveston provides an overview of the port.

Schedule: Open Daily except Thanksgiving and Christmas, 10:00 A.M. to 5:00 P.M.

Admission: Adults $4.00, Seniors $3.00, Children $2.00.

Operation: Passenger train powered by steam locomotive #555 operates on selected dates during year. The 2-mile, ¾-hour trip operates over the Galveston Wharves R.R. along the City's docks.

Locomotives: A partial listing of operable engines:
#555, 2-8-0, Alco (1922), ex-Magma Arizona R.R.
#1303, NW-2 diesel, E.M.D. (1949), ex-Southern Pacific.
#410, H-20-44 diesel, Fairbanks Morse (1947), ex-Union Pacific.
A partial listing of other engines:
#1, 2-6-2, Baldwin (1929), ex-Waco, Trinity, Beaumont & Sabine R.R.
#314, 4-6-0, Cooke (1894), ex-Southern Pacific R.R.
#100, R.D.C. car, Budd (1955), ex-Southern Pacific R.R.

Rolling Stock: Pullman car "Robert E. Lee", (1924); Private Palace Car "Anacapa" (1929); 4 baggage cars housing railroad history exhibits; 11 vintage freight cars; Burlington Zephyr diner "Silver Hours"; Rock Island wrecking train with "big hook"; world's largest tank car, UTLX (1962) and many other locomotives and cars.

Timothy M. Kingsbury, Executive Director

✔Refreshments
✔Gift Shop
✔Memberships

The Center for
Transportation & Commerce
123 Rosenberg
Galveston, TX 77550
Phone (409) 765-5700

Photo by Charlie Maple

Location: The Texas State R.R. runs through the heart of east Texas with Victorian style depots on U.S. 84 near both Rusk and Palestine.

Ride: A 50-mile, 4-hour round trip over a major portion of the original Texas State R.R. built in 1896. Two passenger trains make one round trip each operating day from both Rusk and Palestine.

Schedule: Saturdays & Sundays, March 21 thru May 24 and August 22 thru November 1 (plus Labor Day). Daily (except Tuesdays & Wednesdays), May 25 thru August 16. Train leaves Rusk for Palestine 11:00 A.M., returns 3:00 P.M. Train leaves Palestine for Rusk 11:00 A.M., returns 3:00 P.M. Locomotive tour prior to departure.

Fare: Adults $8.00, Children (3-12) $6.00, under 3 free. (Round trip). Adults $6.00, Children (3-12) $4.00, under 3 free. (One-way). Must arrange own return transportation. Reservations recommended.

Locomotives: #200, 4-6-0, Cooke (1896), ex-Southern Pacific #2248. #201, 4-6-0, Cooke (1901), ex-Texas & Pacific #316. #300, 2-8-0, Baldwin (1917), ex-Texas Southeastern #28. #400, 2-8-2, Baldwin (1917), ex-Magma Arizona #7. #500, 4-6-2, Baldwin (1911), ex-Santa Fe #1316.

Train: Steel combine and six coaches. One open-air coach on each train.

Note: Rusk Depot is located adjacent to the 100-acre Rusk/Palestine State Park, 2½-miles west of Rusk on U.S. 84. Palestine Depot is located 4-miles east of Palestine on U.S. 84. The picnic unit of the State Park is adjacent.

Curtis Pruett, Superintendent

✔Refreshments
✔Gift Shop
✔Picnic Area
✔Ice Cream Parlor on train
✔Camping

Texas State Railroad
P.O. Box 39
Rusk, TX 75785
Phone (214) 683-2563
(800) 442-8951 (In Texas)

Location: The Museum is located in McAllister Park at 11731 Wetmore Road, just north of Interstate 410.

Ride: A short ride in a caboose behind the Museum's spotless Baldwin switch engine or 44-ton diesel. Trackage is still being extended to afford longer rides.

Schedule: Train will operate on the second Sunday of each month, April through October. The Museum is open every Saturday and Sunday, year-round, from 10:00 A.M. to 4:00 P.M., weather permitting.

Fare: Operating days: Adults $2.00, Children $1.00, under 6 free.
Non-operating days: No admission (donations welcomed).

Locomotives: #1, 0-4-0T, Baldwin (1925), ex-Comal Power Co., New Braunfels, TX. #7071, 44-ton diesel, G.E., ex-U.S. Air Force.
#6, 2-8-0, Baldwin (1911), ex-Moscow, Camden & San Augustine R.R. (under restoration).

Train: Locomotive and restored Missouri Pacific caboose #11919.

Displays: Pullman car "McKeever", built in 1924. Southern Pacific station from Converse, Texas; rail cars and artifacts; Santa Fe Business Car #404; 1925 Buffalo fire truck and antique motor vehicles displayed in a new 5,000 sq. ft. pavilion.

Richard Elvey, Chairman

✔Refreshments
✔Picnic Area
✔Memberships

Texas Transportation Museum
11731 Wetmore Road
San Antonio, TX 78247
Phone (512) 490-3554
(512) 227-6453

Amtrak San Antonio

UTAH, HEBER CITY
Heber Creeper Scenic R.R.

Steam, scheduled
Standard gauge

Photo by Steven W. Belmont

Location: Trains depart from Heber City, 46 miles east of Salt Lake City on U.S. 40 or Vivian Park, 11 miles east of Provo on U.S. 189.

Ride: A 32-mile, 3½-hour round trip through the high mountain meadows of the Heber Valley, across rivers and streams and into the deep canyon of the Provo River to Vivian Park.

Schedule: Daily operation, Memorial Day through Labor Day. Week-ends, May 9-24 and November 28-December 27, as well as Daily from December 21 thru 31 (except Christmas Day). Trains depart Heber City at 10:00 A.M. and 2:30 P.M.

Fare: Adults $9.50, Children $5.00, under 3 free.

Locomotives: #264, 2-8-0, Baldwin (1904), ex-Union Pacific R.R.
#618, 2-8-0, Baldwin (1907), ex-Union Pacific R.R.
#1744, 2-6-0, Baldwin (1901), ex-Southern Pacific R.R.
#1000, NW-2 diesel, E.M.D. (1939), ex-Union Pacific R.R.
#1011, NW-2 diesel, E.M.D. (1939), ex-Union Pacific R.R.

Train: Harriman coaches, mountain observation cars and Union Pacific dining car.

Displays: Numerous locomotives and cars may be observed along with a railroad museum in the former D.&R.G.W. depot (circa 1899).

Gloria Montgomery, Manager

✔Refreshments
✔Gift Shops
✔Picnic Area
✔Dining Car

Heber Creeper Scenic R.R.
P.O. Box 103
Heber City, UT 84032
Phone (801) 654-2900
(801) 531-6022

Location: Golden Spike National Historic Site is located 32 miles west of Brigham City, Utah on a marked, paved highway.

Displays: This is the spot where the famous Golden Spike was driven on May 10, 1869, marking the completion of the nation's first transcontinental railroad. Exact operating replicas of the original locomotives are exhibited. In the Visitor Center are color movies and numerous museum exhibits. Park rangers are on hand to explain the importance of the railroad and the significance of the ceremony of 1869.

Schedule: Visitor Center is open Daily, year-round, except closed on winter Federal Holidays. Open from 8:00 A.M. to 4:30 P.M., except June 7 through Labor Day, open from 8:00 A.M. to 5:30 P.M.

Admission: No charge.

Locomotives: Full-size operating replicas of Union Pacific #119 and Central Pacific #60 "Jupiter", both American Standard 4-4-0's. These locomotives are on display on the spot where the Golden Spike was driven. Locomotives are run out on their own power each morning, May through September, returned to the engine house in early evening.

Other: Ranger talks, Big Fill Walk, self-guided auto tour and other activities available. Check the activities board in the Visitor Center.

✔Refreshments
✔Gift Shop
✔Picnic Area

Golden Spike National Historic Site
P.O. Box W
Brigham City, UT 84302
Phone (801) 471-2209

VERMONT, BELLOWS FALLS
Green Mountain Railroad

Diesel, scheduled
Standard gauge

Photo by Jim Shaughnessy

Location: Bellows Falls is located in southern Vermont at the New Hampshire border. The railroad station is located on Depot St. at the junction of the Green Mountain and Boston & Maine Railroads. From Interstate I-91 take Exits 5 or 6.

Ride: A 26-mile, 2-hour round trip from Bellows Falls to Chester, in either direction. Passengers may continue on to Ludlow for a 54-mile round trip. New Ludlow to Chester trains offer a 28-mile round trip. This line was once the route of the famed Rutland Railroad.

Schedule: Bellows Falls to Chester: Daily, June 20 thru September 7 plus September 26 thru October 12. Week-ends, September 12-20 & October 17-25. Lv. Bellows Falls 11:00 A.M., 1:30, *3:50 P.M. Lv. Chester 12:10, *2:40 P.M. Ludlow service, week-ends only, July 18-August 30 and September 26-October 12. Lv. Ludlow at 1:00 P.M. (* week-ends only)

Fare: Bellows Falls-Chester: Adults $7.00, Children (5-12) $4.00.
Bellows Falls-Ludlow: Adults $16.00, Children (5-12) $8.00.
Ludlow-Chester: Adults $10.00, Children (5-12) $5.00.
Children under 5 free. One-way fares and group rates available.

Locomotives: #400, 401, 405, RS-1 diesels, Alco. #405, ex-Rutland R.R., #400, 401, ex-Illinois Terminal. #1849, GP-9 diesel, EMD, ex-Burlington Northern.

Train: Restored open-window coaches from Rutland R.R. and Jersey Central.

Note: Tickets are sold at Bellows Falls Union Station and on all trains. In Chester, at Vermont Marble, Munroe Market and Cummings Hardware. In Ludlow at the Chamber of Commerce office. The Green Mountain Railroad is a working freight line.

✔Gift Shop

Green Mountain Railroad
P.O. Box 498
Bellows Falls, VT 05101
Phone (802) 463-3069

Photo by James R. Dufour

Location: The Lamoille Valley R.R. operates a 128 mile rail route through northern Vermont. Scheduled passenger excursion trains run from Morrisville east through spectacular Green Mountain scenery. The site is only 10 miles from Stowe and near Mt. Mansfield, Vermont's highest peak.

Ride: A 70-mile, 4½-hour round trip from Morrisville to Joe's Pond and return. The train follows the winding course of the Lamoille River, passes through one of the country's last covered railroad bridges and negotiates a long and unusual horseshoe curve up Walden Mountain. Train pauses for a ¾-hour lunch stop at Joe's Pond before beginning its return journey.

Schedule: From June 27 through August 29, trains leave Morrisville on Tuesdays, Thursdays and Saturdays at 10:00 A.M., return at 2:30 P.M. From September 19 through October 18, Fall Foliage trains operate a shorter run, leaving Morrisville on Tuesdays, Thursdays, Saturdays and Sundays at 10:00 A.M. and 2:00 P.M.

Fare: Regular trains: Adults $15.00, Children (5-13) $10.00.
Fall Foliage: Adults $12.00, Children (5-13) $8.00.
Reservations suggested. Visa and Mastercard accepted.

Locomotives: #7801, 7803, 7804, RS-3 diesels, Alco (1952), ex-Delaware & Hudson. Also #117, #144, Alco RS-3 diesels, ex-Amtrak.

Train: Open-window coaches from Delaware, Lackawanna & Western R.R..

Note: The Lamoille Valley is a working common-carrier railroad.

✔Refreshments
✔Picnic Stop

Lamoille Valley Railroad
Stafford Avenue
Morrisville, VT 05661
Phone (802) 888-4255

Photo by Shelburne Museum, Inc.

Location: The Museum is located 7 miles south of Burlington, Vt. on U.S. Route 7.

Displays: The Shelburne Museum displays an extensive and internationally renowned collection of Americana. Exhibits are housed in 37 historic buildings on a 45-acre site. The railroad exhibit features the restored 1890 Shelburne depot with a Central Vermont steam locomotive and the private car "Grand Isle." Nearby is housed the steam inspection car "Gertie Buck" from the Woodstock R.R. There is also a wooden replica of Baldwin's "Old Ironsides" of 1832 and a collection of railroad memorabilia. Other exhibits at the Museum include a 220 ft. sidewheel steamer, S.S. Ticonderoga, which was moved overland from Lake Champlain, collections of antiques, quilts, carriages, art, decoys and tools. This year Shelburne will have an authentic carousel in daily operation.

Locomotives: #220, 4-6-0, Alco (1915), ex-Central Vermont Ry.

Schedule: Museum is open Daily, May 16 through October 18, 1987 from 9:00 A.M. to 5:00 P.M.

Admission: Adults $9.50, Children (6-17) $4.00, under 6 free.
Group rates available. Limited handicapped access.

Benjamin L. Mason, Director

✔Refreshments
✔Museum Shop
✔Picnic Area
✔Restaurant

Shelburne Museum
Shelburne, VT 05482
Phone (802) 985-3344

175

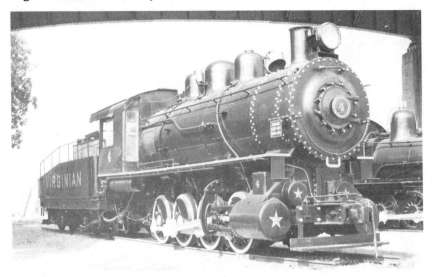

Displays: The Virginia Museum of Transportation (formerly the Roanoke Transportation Museum) is the Official Transportation Museum of the Commonwealth of Virginia. On exhibit are a number of steam, diesel and electric locomotives and an extensive collection of passenger cars, freight cars, cabooses, trolleys and a great deal of memorabilia. The Museum has been relocated from its former site to a 1917 Norfolk & Western Freight Station.

Schedule: Open Daily from 10:00 A.M. to 5:00 P.M., Sundays from Noon to 5:00 P.M. Closed Thanksgiving, Christmas and New Year's Day.

Admission: Adults $2.00, Seniors $1.60, Children (3-12) $1.00, under 3 free. Group rates available. Prices subject to change.

Locomotives: #4, 0-8-0, Class SA, Baldwin (1910), Virginian Ry.
#6, 2-8-0, Class G-1, Baldwin (1897), Norfolk & Western Ry.
#763, 2-8-4, Class S-2, Lima (1944), Nickel Plate Road.
#1604, 2-6-6-6, Class H-8, Lima (1941), Chesapeake & Ohio Ry.

Other Displays: P.C.C. trolley from Washington, DC; N.&W. dynamometer car; Norfolk & Western's first diesel; Illinois Terminal R.R. business car and many other railroad displays. There are also old automobiles and trucks on exhibit. Write for free brochure.

Note: Two locomotives from the Museum's collection have been re-habilitated and placed in excursion train service by the Norfolk Southern. N.&W. Class J 4-8-4 No. 611 is in operation, while giant Class A 2-6-6-4 No. 1218 will enter excursion service in the Spring of 1987.

Nancy M. McBride, Executive Director

✔Gift Shop

Virginia Museum of Transportation
303 Norfolk Ave., S.W.
Roanoke, VA 24016
Phone (703) 342-5670

Photo courtesy Norfolk Southern Corp.

Ride: Day-long or two-day excursion trains will operate over many lines of the Norfolk Southern again this year. Trips will operate over lines of the Southern Railway and Norfolk & Western Ry. All trips will be sponsored by on-line chapters of the National Railway Historical Society, railway museums, railroad and civic groups.

Schedule: Norfolk Southern's excursion train service for 1987 will run from March 28 to November 22. Three steam locomotives will operate, augmented in some cases by diesel power. Famous Norfolk & Western Class J #611, newly overhauled N.&W. Class A #1218 articulated and Kentucky Railway Museum's light Pacific #152 will power excursion trains. Diesel trips will utilize Southern Ry. FP-7's or other diesels.

Fare: Determined by trip. Tickets must be purchased from trip sponsors.

Locomotives: #611, 4-8-4, Class J, Roanoke Shops (1950), N.&W. Ry.
#1218, 2-6-6-4, Class A, Roanoke Shops (1943), N.&W. Ry.
#152, 4-6-2, Rogers (1905), ex-Louisville & Nashville R.R.

Train: Air-conditioned and open-window coaches, commissary cars and specially built open-sided observation cars. Some trains include deluxe, first-class cars.

Note: For information, schedules and fares for specific trips, please write to trip sponsors shown on following pages.

Carl S. Jensen
Manager, Steam Operations
Norfolk Southern Corp.
8 N. Jefferson St.
Roanoke, VA 24042-0002

✔Refreshments on train
✔Gift Shop on train

NORFOLK SOUTHERN

STEAM SCHEDULE — MAY 23 - NOV. 22, 1987

Norfolk Southern's 1987 Steam and Diesel Excursion Train Schedule is shown below. While trips began on March 28, the schedule prior to May 23 has been omitted to conserve space. Please contact Trip Sponsors directly for train schedules, reservations and ticket information.
(RT = Round Trip) (OW = One-way)

DATE			LOCO.	SPONSOR
May 23	Greenville, SC - Toccoa, GA	RT	1218	GVN
24	Greenville, SC - Kannapolis, NC (Diesel return)	RT	1218	GVN
30	Knoxville, TN - Natural Tunnel, VA	RT	152	OS
30	Salisbury, NC - Asheville, NC	RT	1218	NCTH
31	Salisbury, NC area circle trip		Diesel	NCTH
June 6	Charlotte, NC - Spartanburg, SC	RT	1218	PCCN
6	Bristol, VA - Walton, VA	RT	152	WTC
7	Johnson City, TN - Natural Tunnel, VA	RT	152	WTC
7	Charlotte, NC - Greensboro, NC (Diesel return)	RT	1218	PCCN
13	Greensboro, NC - Lynchburg, VA (Diesel return)	RT	1218	GCN
13	Knoxville, TN - Asheville, NC	OW	152	MSS
14	Asheville, NC - Knoxville, TN	OW	152	MSS
26	Detroit, MI - Chicago, IL	OW	611	BWC
27	Chicago, IL - Fort Wayne, IN	RT	611	CNRH
28	Chicago, IL - Detroit, MI	OW	611	BWC
July 11	Detroit, MI - Fort Wayne, IN	RT	611	BWC
12	Detroit, MI - Fort Wayne, IN	RT	611	BWC
11-12	Huntingburg, IN area		152	MCH
18	Cincinnati, OH - Portsmouth, OH (Diesel return)	RT	611	CCN
18-19	Alexandria, VA area 1218 and FP-7's			WACN
25-26	Alexandria, VA area 1218 and FP-7's			WACN
July 29 -	Roanoke, VA area - NRHS National Convention			RCN
Aug. 2	611 - 1218 - FP-7's			
Aug. 8	Kenova, WV - Columbus, OH	RT	1218	CPHC
8	Charlotte, NC - Atlanta, GA	OW	611	DP
9	Atlanta, GA - Charlotte, NC	OW	Diesel	DP
15	Toledo, OH - Columbus, OH	RT	1218	MRC
16	Bellevue, OH - Columbus, OH	RT	1218	MRC
Sept. 12-13	Cincinnati, OH - Danville, KY	RT	1218	CCN
19	Lexington, KY - Chattanooga, TN	OW	1218	BGM
20	Chattanooga, TN - Lexington, KY	OW	1218	BGM
Oct. 10	Hagerstown, MD - Luray, VA	RT	FP-7's	WC
17-18	Chattanooga, TN - Crossville, TN	RT	1218	TVRM
17-18	Roanoke, VA - Abingdon, VA	RT	FP-7's	RCN
24-25	Chattanooga, TN - Crossville, TN	RT	Diesel	TVRM
24	Asheville, NC - Hickory, NC	RT	FP-7's	ASHV
25	Asheville, NC - Bulls Gap, TN	RT	FP-7's	ASHV
31	Atlanta, GA - Chattanooga, TN	RT	1218	ACN
Nov. 1	Atlanta, GA - Toccoa, GA	RT	1218	ACN
7	Atlanta, GA - Chattanooga, TN	RT	1218	ACN
8	Atlanta, GA - Toccoa, GA	RT	1218	ACN
14-15	Jacksonville, FL - Valdosta, GA	RT	1218	NFC
21-22	Jacksonville, FL - Valdosta, GA	RT	1218	NFC

NORFOLK SOUTHERN

SPONSORS

ACN	Atlanta Chapter, NRHS P.O. Box 14157 Atlanta, GA 30337	MRC	Mad River & NKP R.R. Soc. P.O. Box 42 Bellevue, OH 44811
ASHV	Asheville Chapter, NRHS c/o Antique Train & Toy Co. 640 Merrimon Ave. Asheville, NC 28804	MSS	Natl. Multiple Sclerosis Soc. Suburban Office Plaza, Suite 109 301 Gallaher View Road Knoxville, TN 37919
BGM	Bluegrass Railroad Museum P.O. Box 1711 Lexington, KY 40592	NCTH	North Carolina Trans. History P.O. Box 44 Spencer, NC 28159
BWC	Bluewater Michigan Chapter, NRHS P.O. Box 296 Royal Oak, MI 48068	NFC	North Florida Chapter, NRHS P.O. Box 16493 Jacksonville, FL 32245
CCN	Cincinnati Railroad Club P.O. Box 36060 Cincinnati, OH 45214	OS	Old Smoky Chapter, NRHS P.O. Box 601 Knoxville, TN 37901
CNRH	Chicago Chapter, NRHS 5246 South Newland Chicago, IL 60638	PCCN	Piedmont Carolinas Chapter, NRHS 3741 Larkston Drive Charlotte, NC 28226
CPHC	C.P. Huntington Chapter, NRHS P.O. Box 271 Huntington, WV 25707	RCN	Roanoke Chapter, NRHS P.O. Box 13222 Roanoke, VA 24032
DP	Discovery Place/Science Museum 301 N. Tryon St. Charlotte, NC 28202	TVRM	Tennessee Valley R.R. Museum 4119 Cromwell Road Chattanooga, TN 37421
GCN	Greensboro Chapter, NRHS P.O. Box 16745 Greensboro, NC 27406	WACN	Washington Area Chapter, NRHS Chesapeake R.R. Enthusiasts P.O. Box 456 Laurel, MD 20707
GVN	Greenville Chapter, NRHS P.O. Box 5481 Greenville, SC 29606	WC	Winchester Chapter, NRHS 29 Whites Place Winchester, VA 22601
MCH	Mayor's Committee Mayor Dale Helmerich Huntingburg, IN 47542	WTC	Watuaga Valley Chapter, NRHS P.O. Box 432 Johnson City, TN 37605

Photo by Dave Wilkie

Location: Elbe is located on Highway #7, 40 miles east of Tacoma on the main route to Mt. Rainier National Park.

Ride: A 14-mile, 1½-hour round trip over scenic trackage on the south slope of Mt. Rainier. Travel past farms, tall timber preserves and over 2 bridges crossing the Nisqually River with beautiful views of the mountain. Train stops 20 minutes at Mineral Lake where antique logging equipment may be viewed. Passengers may stop-over and return on a later train. Once each month a special train will run to Morton, a 34-mile, 4-hour round trip. Call or write for details.

Schedule: Week-ends, Memorial Day through September 20. Daily, June 15 through Labor Day. Trains leave Elbe at 11:00 A.M., 1:15 & 3:30 P.M.

Fare: Adults $6.50, Seniors $5.50, Juniors (12-16) $4.50, Children (under 12) $3.50, Family $17.00.

Locomotives: #5, 2-8-2, Porter (1924), ex-Port of Grays Harbor.
#10, 3-truck Climax (1928), ex-Hillcrest Lumber Co.
#91, West Coast Special Heisler (1930), ex-Kinzua Pine Mills.
#41, RSD-1 diesel, Alco (1941), ex-Dept. of Transportation.
#7012A, F-9 diesel, E.M.D. (1956), ex-Northern Pacific R.R.

Display Locomotives: #11, Pacific Coast Shay (1928), ex-Pickering Lumber.
#12, 3-truck Heisler (1912), ex-Pickering Lumber Co.
#17, 2-8-2T, Alco (1929), ex-Hammond Lumber Co.

Train: Commuter coaches with windows that open and open -air observation cars. All trains feature live music on board.

Note: Special excursions, Spring and Fall, over main-line of Chehalis Western. Call or write for details.

🡒Gift Shop
🡒Picnic Area
🡒Restaurant
🡒RV Parking

Mt. Rainier Scenic R.R.
P.O. Box 921
Elbe, WA 98330
Phone (206) 569-2588

WASHINGTON, SNOQUALMIE
Puget Sound & Snoqualmie Valley R.R.

Steam, Diesel, scheduled
Standard gauge

Location: Trains depart from depot in Snoqualmie or from North Bend's new depot (opens mid-season). The site is 30 miles east of Seattle on I-90, use Exits 27 or 31. May also be reached by Metro bus #210.

Ride: A scenic 10-mile, 1 hour round trip between North Bend, Snoqualmie and Snoqualmie Falls.

Schedule: Sundays, April thru October. Saturdays, Memorial Day week-end thru October, plus Memorial Day and Labor Day. Trains depart Snoqualmie 11:01 A.M., 12:31, 2:01 & 3:31 P.M., depart North Bend 30 minutes later. Additional train leaves Snoqualmie at 5:01 P.M. on weekends Memorial Day thru Labor Day.

Fare: Adults $5.00, Seniors (62+) $4.00, Children (3-12) $3.00.

Locomotives: #11, 2-6-6-2, Baldwin (1926), ex-U.S. Plywood Corp. Diesels include: #909, Alco RSD-4, ex-Kennecott Copper Co.; P.T.S. #121, Fairbanks-Morse H12-44; #7320, 45-ton General Electric, ex-U.S. Navy.

Train: Heavyweight equipment, including ex-Union Pacific observation car.

Displays: There are over 100 pieces of railway equipment in the Museum's collection. Locomotives, passenger and freight cars, traction equipment, logging and work cars are all represented.

✔Gift Shop
✔Picnic Area
✔Memberships

 Seattle

Puget Sound Railway Hist. Assn.
P.O. Box 459
Snoqualmie, WA 98065
Phone (206) 746-4025 (24-hr. number)
(206) 888-3030 (operating hours)

181

Photo by Tim J. Johnson

Location: The Camp Six Logging Exhibit is located on Five Mile Drive in Point Defiance Park.

Ride: The Exhibit is in the only natural forest in a city park in the nation. The entire project is laid out to represent an authentic old-time logging camp, with all exhibits having been in actual use by loggers. The Point Defiance, Quinault & Klickitat R.R. operates over a 1½-mile track with the trip taking about 15 minutes.

Schedule: Operates Memorial Day through Labor Day, Saturdays, Sundays and Holidays only. Continuous trips dependent on arrival of passengers, from 11:00 A.M. to 6:00 P.M. During summer months a speeder is operated on weekdays and weekends before and after steam runs.

Fare: Steam Train: Adults $1.50, Children 75¢, Seniors 75¢.

Locomotives: #7, 3-truck Pacific Coast Shay, Lima (1929), ex-St. Regis Paper Co.

Train: Flatcar equipped with benches.

Displays: Lidgerwood Skidder, five car mobile car camp, five-car loaded log train, Dolbeer donkey, Yarding & Loading donkeys, 110 ft. rigged Spar Tree. Two buildings filled with historic logging pictures and artifacts.

Tom Nosera, Curator

✔Picnic Area

 Tacoma

Camp Six Logging Exhibit
Point Defiance Park
Tacoma, WA 98407
Phone (206) 752-0047

Photo by Dale Campbell

Location: Steam trains leave from Wickersham on N.P. Road. The site is in extreme northwestern Washington near Bellingham on Highway 9.

Ride: A 7-mile, 1¼-hour round trip over a former Northern Pacific branch line. The train climbs a 2.4% grade along Highway 9 and then heads through the forest. The route was constructed as the Bellingham Bay & Eastern R.R. and later became the Northern Pacific's Bellingham branch.

Schedule: Steam trains operate Saturdays and Tuesdays, June 6 through August 29. Lv. Wickersham Noon and 2:00 P.M. Trains also run Saturdays in December (reservations required). Note: additional trains will operate from Park during the summer. Call or write for information.

Fare: Adults $6.00, Juniors (17 & under) $3.00.
Charter trips available at all times, including use of parlor car.

Locomotives: #1070, 0-6-0, Alco (1907), ex-Northern Pacific Ry.

Train: Northern Pacific heavyweight passenger cars. "Mainstreeter" coffee shop car.

Displays: Northern Pacific business car "Madison River". 1923 Shell Oil Co. tank car, old Great Northern boxcars, 1909 N.P. wooden caboose.

✔Refreshments on train
✔Gift Shop
✔Picnic Area
✔Camping

Lake Whatcom Railway
P.O. Box 91
Acme, WA 98220
Phone (206) 595-2218

 Seattle
Everett

183

Ride: Cass Scenic R.R. operates over a reconstructed logging railroad which saw 60 years of actual service. The line, operated by the State of West Virginia, climbs grades as steep as 11% and features 2 switchbacks. The overlooks and panoramas of the mountain scenery are unrivaled in the east. Passengers may choose either the 22-mile, 4½-hour round trip to the top of Bald Knob (elevation 4842 ft.) or the shorter 8-mile, 1½-hour round trip to Whittaker Station.

Schedule: Daily, May 23 through Labor Day.

Week-ends only in September and October. No Bald Knob train on Mondays.

To Whittaker: Lv. Cass *11:00 A.M., 1:00 & 3:00 P.M. (* begins July)
To Bald Knob: Lv. Cass 12:00 Noon.

Special Saturday evening Dinner Trains on May 30, June 13 & 27, July 11 & 25, Aug. 8 & 29, lv. 6:00 P.M. Reservations required, call for information.

Fare: To Whittaker: Adults $7.00, Children $3.00.
To Bald Knob: Adults $9.50, Children $4.00.
Dinner Train: Adults $20.00, Children $15.00.

Locomotives: #2, 3-truck Shay, Lima (1928); #3, 3-truck Shay, Lima (1923); #4, 3-truck Shay, Lima (1922); #5, 3-truck Shay, Lima (1905); #6, 3-truck Heisler (1929); Western Maryland #6, 3-truck, 162-ton Shay, Lima (1945); #7, 3-truck Shay, Lima (1921); #8, 3-truck Climax (1919); #612, 2-8-0, Baldwin (1943); #20, 45-ton diesel, G.E. (1941); #7172, BL-2 diesel, EMD (1948), ex-Western Maryland No. 82.

Train: Former logging cars converted for passenger use.

Displays: Modern steam locomotive shop complex open for inspection on week-days.

Note: Advance reservations for trips on Cass Scenic R.R. not accepted. Special group rates available Tuesdays through Fridays. Charter rates available upon request.

Fred Bartels, Superintendent

✔Refreshments
✔Gift Shop
✔Picnic Area
✔Restaurant
✔Camping Area
✔Lodging

Cass Scenic Railroad
Cass, WV 24927
Phone (304) 456-4300
1-800-CALL-WVA
456-4362 (after 5 P.M.)

STEAM PASSENGER DIRECTORY 1987 GUEST COUPONS

Savings for you and your family shown on reverse side of coupon

LOMITA RAILROAD MUSEUM
LOMITA, CALIFORNIA
Steam Passenger Directory
1987 Guest Coupon

TRAVEL TOWN RAILROAD
LOS ANGELES, CALIFORNIA
Steam Passenger Directory
1987 Guest Coupon

TRAIN TOWN
SONOMA, CALIFORNIA
Steam Passenger Directory
1987 Guest Coupon

CRIPPLE CREEK NARROW GAUGE R.R.
CRIPPLE CREEK, COLORADO
Steam Passenger Directory
1987 Guest Coupon

FORNEY HISTORIC TRANSPORTATION MUSEUM
DENVER, COLORADO
Steam Passenger Directory
1987 Guest Coupon

COLORADO RAILROAD MUSEUM
GOLDEN, COLORADO
Steam Passenger Directory
1987 Guest Coupon

SHORE LINE TROLLEY MUSEUM
EAST HAVEN, CONNECTICUT
Steam Passenger Directory
1987 Guest Coupon

VALLEY RAILROAD COMPANY
ESSEX, CONNECTICUT
Steam Passenger Directory
1987 Guest Coupon

WILMINGTON & WESTERN RAILROAD
WILMINGTON, DELAWARE
Steam Passenger Directory
1987 Guest Coupon

GOLD COAST RAILROAD MUSEUM
MIAMI, FLORIDA
Steam Passenger Directory
1987 Guest Coupon

1987 GUEST COUPONS

Savings Available And Conditions For Use

TRAVEL TOWN RAILROAD
Regular Fare: Adults $1.50, Children $1.25
WITH THIS COUPON: Adults & Children 75¢
Valid until April 1988

LOMITA RAILROAD MUSEUM
Regular Admission: Adults & Children 50¢
WITH THIS COUPON: Adults & Children 25¢
Valid from June 1987 to June 1988

CRIPPLE CREEK NARROW GAUGE R.R.
Regular Fare: Adults $4.75, Children $2.75
WITH THIS COUPON: 50¢ off Adults & Children
Valid until October 9, 1987

TRAIN TOWN
Regular Fare: Adults $2.20, Children $1.60
WITH THIS COUPON: Adults $1.10, Children 80¢
Valid during 1987

COLORADO RAILROAD MUSEUM
Regular Admission: Adults $2.50,
Children $1.00
WITH THIS COUPON: Adults $2.00, Children 75¢
Valid during 1987

FORNEY HISTORIC TRANSPORTATION MUSEUM
Regular Admission: Adults $3.00, Children
(12-18) $1.50, (5-11) 50¢
WITH THIS COUPON: One free admission with
one paid Adult admission
Valid from May 1987 to May 1988

VALLEY RAILROAD COMPANY
Regular Fare: Adults $6.95, Children $2.95
WITH THIS COUPON: Adults & Children less 10%
Valid during 1987

SHORE LINE TROLLEY MUSEUM
Regular Fare: Adults $3.50, Children $1.50
WITH THIS COUPON: 50¢ off Adults & Children
Valid until November 22, 1987

GOLD COAST RAILROAD MUSEUM
Regular Fare: Adults $4.25, Children $2.25
WITH THIS COUPON: Adults $3.25, Children $1.75
Valid during 1987

WILMINGTON & WESTERN RAILROAD
Regular Fare: Adults $5.00, Children $3.00
WITH THIS COUPON: $1.00 off Adults &Children
Valid until October 31, 1987

STEAM PASSENGER DIRECTORY 1987 GUEST COUPONS

Savings for you and your family shown on reverse side of coupon

HART COUNTY SCENIC RAILWAY
HARTWELL, GEORGIA
Steam Passenger Directory
1987 Guest Coupon

BIG SHANTY MUSEUM
KENNESAW, GEORGIA
Steam Passenger Directory
1987 Guest Coupon

WHITEWATER VALLEY RAILROAD
CONNERSVILLE, INDIANA
Steam Passenger Directory
1987 Guest Coupon

MIDWEST CENTRAL RAILROAD
Mt. PLEASANT, IOWA
Steam Passenger Directory
1987 Guest Coupon

KENTUCKY RAILWAY MUSEUM
LOUISVILLE, KENTUCKY
Steam Passenger Directory
1987 Guest Coupon

B.& O. RAILROAD MUSEUM
BALTIMORE, MARYLAND
Steam Passenger Directory
1987 Guest Coupon

BALTIMORE STREETCAR MUSEUM
BALTIMORE, MARYLAND
Steam Passenger Directory
1987 Guest Coupon

NATIONAL CAPITAL TROLLEY MUSEUM
WHEATON, MARYLAND
Steam Passenger Directory
1987 Guest Coupon

A.& D. TOY TRAIN VILLAGE
MIDDLEBORO, MASSACHUSETTS
Steam Passenger Directory
1987 Guest Coupon

EDAVILLE RAILROAD
SOUTH CARVER, MASSACHUSETTS
Steam Passenger Directory
1987 Guest Coupon

1987 GUEST COUPONS

Savings Available And Conditions For Use

BIG SHANTY MUSEUM
Regular Fare: Adults $2.00, Children 50¢
WITH THIS COUPON: Adults $1.00
Valid during 1987

HART COUNTY SCENIC RAILWAY
Regular Fare: Adults $5.00, Children $3.00
WITH THIS COUPON: $1.00 off Adults & Children
Valid until October 4, 1987

MIDWEST CENTRAL RAILROAD
Regular Fare: Adults $1.50, Children 75¢
WITH THIS COUPON: Adults 75¢, Children 40¢
Valid September 3-7, 1987

WHITEWATER VALLEY RAILROAD
Regular Fare: Adults $8.00, Children $4.00
WITH THIS COUPON: Adults $7.00, Children $3.50
Valid until November 1, 1987

B.& O. RAILROAD MUSEUM
Regular Admission: Adults $2.50, Children $1.50
WITH THIS COUPON: 50¢ off Adults & Children
Valid during 1987

KENTUCKY RAILWAY MUSEUM
Regular Admission: Adults $2.00, Seniors & Children $1.5
WITH THIS COUPON: Adults $1.50, Seniors & Children $1.25
Valid until October 31, 1987

NATIONAL CAPITAL TROLLEY MUSEUM
Regular Fare: Adults $1.00, Children under 18, 75¢
WITH THIS COUPON: One free Adult's
plus one free Child's fare
Valid until June 30, 1988

BALTIMORE STREETCAR MUSEUM
Regular Fare: Adults $1.00, Children (4-11) 50¢
WITH THIS COUPON: 1 free ride with paid fare
of equal or greater value
Valid until April 30, 1988

EDAVILLE RAILROAD
Regular Fare: Adults $7.50, Children $5.00
WITH THIS COUPON: $1.00 off Adults & Children
Valid until January 3, 1988

A.& D. TOY TRAIN VILLAGE
Regular Admission: Adults $3.00, Children $1.50
WITH THIS COUPON: Adults $2.40, Children $1.20
Valid until March 31, 1988

STEAM PASSENGER DIRECTORY 1987 GUEST COUPONS

Savings for your family shown on reverse side of coupon

HUCKLEBERRY RAILROAD
FLINT, MICHIGAN
Steam Passenger Directory
1987 Guest Coupon

MICHIGAN TRANSIT MUSEUM
MT. CLEMENS, MICHIGAN
Steam Passenger Directory
1987 Guest Coupon

WABASH FRISCO & PACIFIC RY.
GLENCOE, MISSOURI
Steam Passenger Directory
1987 Guest Coupon

NATIONAL MUSEUM OF TRANSPORT
ST. LOUIS, MISSOURI
Steam Passenger Directory
1987 Guest Coupon

WINNIPESAUKEE RAILROAD
MEREDITH, NEW HAMPSHIRE
Steam Passenger Directory
1987 Guest Coupon

CONWAY SCENIC RAILROAD
NORTH CONWAY, NEW HAMPSHIRE
Steam Passenger Directory
1987 Guest Coupon

ARCADE & ATTICA R.R.
ARCADE, NEW YORK
Steam Passenger Directory
1987 Guest Coupon

DELAWARE & ULSTER RAIL RIDE
ARKVILLE, NEW YORK
Steam Passenger Directory
1987 Guest Coupon

TIOGA CENTRAL RAIL EXCURSIONS
OWEGO, NEW YORK
Steam Passenger Directory
1987 Guest Coupon

TWEETSIE RAILROAD
BLOWING ROCK, NORTH CAROLINA
Steam Passenger Directory
1987 Guest Coupon

1987 GUEST COUPONS

Savings Available And Conditions For Use

MICHIGAN TRANSIT MUSEUM
Regular Fare: Adults $3.00, Children $1.75
WITH THIS COUPON: Adults $2.00, Children $1.00
Valid until September 27, 1987

HUCKLEBERRY RAILROAD
Regular Fare: Adults $5.95, Children $3.95
WITH THIS COUPON: Adults $4.75, Children $3.15
Valid until September 7, 1987

NATIONAL MUSEUM OF TRANSPORT
Regular Admission: Adults $2.00, Children $1.00
WITH THIS COUPON: Buy one, get one free
(Of equal or lesser value)
Valid until March 1, 1988

WABASH FRISCO & PACIFIC RY.
Regular Fare: Adults & Children $1.50
WITH THIS COUPON: Adults & Children $1.00
Valid until June 30, 1988

CONWAY SCENIC RAILROAD
Regular Fare: Adults $5.00, Children (4-12) $3.00
WITH THIS COUPON: 50¢ off Adults & Children
(Maximum two persons per coupon)
Valid until October 25, 1987

WINNIPESAUKEE RAILROAD
Regular Fare: Adults $6.00, Children $4.00
WITH THIS COUPON: 50¢ off Adults & Children
(Maximum two persons per coupon)
Valid until September 20, 1987

DELAWARE & ULSTER RAIL RIDE
Regular Fare: Adults $5.00, Children $2.50
WITH THIS COUPON: Adults $4.50, Children $2.25
Valid until November 1, 1987

ARCADE & ATTICA R.R.
Regular Fare: Adults $5.00, Children $3.00
WITH THIS COUPON: Adults $4.50, Children $2.75
Valid until October 31, 1987

TWEETSIE RAILROAD
Regular Fare: Adults $9.00, Children $7.00
WITH THIS COUPON: $1.00 off Adults & Children
Valid until October 25, 1987

TIOGA CENTRAL RAIL EXCURSIONS
Regular Fare: Adults $4.50, Children $2.50
WITH THIS COUPON: $1.00 off Adults & Children
Valid until November 22, 1987

STEAM PASSENGER DIRECTORY 1987 GUEST COUPONS

Savings for you and your family shown on reverse side of coupon

INDIANA & OHIO RAILROAD
MASON, OHIO
Steam Passenger Directory
1987 Guest Coupon

BUCKEYE CENTRAL SCENIC RAILROAD
NEWARK, OHIO
Steam Passenger Directory
1987 Guest Coupon

TOLEDO, LAKE ERIE & WESTERN RY.
WATERVILLE, OHIO
Steam Passenger Directory
1987 Guest Coupon

RAILROADERS MEMORIAL MUSEUM
ALTOONA, PENNSYLVANIA
Steam Passenger Directory
1987 Guest Coupon

PIONEER TUNNEL COAL MINE R.R.
ASHLAND, PENNSYLVANIA
Steam Passenger Directory
1987 Guest Coupon

BELLEFONTE HISTORICAL RAILROAD
BELLEFONTE, PENNSYLVANIA
Steam Passenger Directory
1987 Guest Coupon

GETTYSBURG RAILROAD
GETTYSBURG, PENNSYLVANIA
Steam Passenger Directory
1987 Guest Coupon

WANAMAKER, KEMPTON & SOUTHERN R.R.
KEMPTON, PENNSYLVANIA
Steam Passenger Directory
1987 Guest Coupon

WEST SHORE RAIL EXCURSIONS
MIFFLINBURG, PENNSYLVANIA
Steam Passenger Directory
1987 Guest Coupon

SHADE GAP ELECTRIC RAILWAY
ORBISONIA, PENNSYLVANIA
Steam Passenger Directory
1987 Guest Coupon

1987 GUEST COUPONS

Savings Available And Conditions For Use

BUCKEYE CENTRAL SCENIC RAILROAD
Regular Fare: Adults $3.00, Children $2.00
WITH THIS COUPON: 50¢ off Adults & Children
Valid during 1987

INDIANA & OHIO RAILROAD
Regular Fare: Adults $7.00, Children $3.50
WITH THIS COUPON: Adults $6.00, Children $3.00
(Maximum 4 persons per coupon)
Valid until November 1, 1987

RAILROADERS MEMORIAL MUSEUM
Regular Admission: Adults $2.50, Children $1.00
WITH THIS COUPON: 50¢ off Adults & Children
Valid until March 31, 1988

TOLEDO, LAKE ERIE & WESTERN RY.
Regular Fare: Adults $5.90, Children $2.95
WITH THIS COUPON: Adults $5.30, Children $2.65
Valid until November 1, 1987

BELLEFONTE HISTORICAL RAILROAD
Regular Fare: Adults $3.00, Children $2.00
WITH THIS COUPON: $1.00 off Adults & Children
Valid until September 27, 1987

PIONEER TUNNEL COAL MINE R.R.
WITH THIS COUPON: 10% discount on all paid admissions
Valid until October 31, 1987

WANAMAKER, KEMPTON & SOUTHERN R.R
Regular Fare: Adults $2.50, Children $1.25
WITH THIS COUPON: Adults $2.00, Children $1.00
Valid until October 31, 1987

GETTYSBURG RAILROAD
Regular Fare: Adults $4.50, Children $3.00
WITH THIS COUPON: 50¢ off Adults & Children
Valid from June 1 to October 31, 1987

SHADE GAP ELECTRIC RAILWAY
Regular Fare: Adults. Children $1.50
WITH THIS COUPON: One free Pass good
for one day
Valid until November 1, 1987

WEST SHORE RAIL EXCURSIONS
Regular Fare: Adults $5.00 & $3.00.
Children $2.00 & $1.50
WITH THIS COUPON: 50¢ off Adults & Children
Valid until November 1, 1987

STEAM PASSENGER DIRECTORY 1987 GUEST COUPONS

Savings for you and your family shown on reverse side of coupon

PENN'S LANDING TROLLEY
PHILADELPHIA, PENNSYLVANIA
Steam Passenger Directory
1987 Guest Coupon

STEAMTOWN, U.S.A.
SCRANTON, PENNSYLVANIA
Steam Passenger Directory
1987 Guest Coupon

RAILROAD MUSEUM OF PENNSYLVANIA
STRASBURG, PENNSYLVANIA
Steam Passenger Directory
1987 Guest Coupon

TOY TRAIN MUSEUM
STRASBURG, PENNSYLVANIA
Steam Passenger Directory
1987 Guest Coupon

OIL CREEK & TITUSVILLE RAILROAD
TITUSVILLE, PENNSYLVANIA
Steam Passenger Directory
1987 Guest Coupon

TENNESSEE VALLEY RAILROAD MUSEUM
CHATTANOOGA, TENNESSEE
Steam Passenger Directory
1987 Guest Coupon

"AGE OF STEAM" RAILROAD MUSEUM
DALLAS, TEXAS
Steam Passenger Directory
1987 Guest Coupon

CENTER FOR TRANSPORTATION & COMMERCE
GALVESTON, TEXAS
Steam Passenger Directory
1987 Guest Coupon

HEBER CREEPER SCENIC R.R.
HEBER CITY, UTAH
Steam Passenger Directory
1987 Guest Coupon

GREEN MOUNTAIN RAILROAD
BELLOWS FALLS, VERMONT
Steam Passenger Directory
1987 Guest Coupon

1987 GUEST COUPONS

Savings Available And Conditions For Use

STEAMTOWN, U.S.A.
Regular Fare: Varies with trip
WITH THIS COUPON: $1.00 off Adults & Children
Valid until November 1, 1987

PENN'S LANDING TROLLEY
Regular Fare: Adults $1.50, Children 50¢
WITH THIS COUPON: 25¢ off Adults & Children
Valid until December 6, 1987

TOY TRAIN MUSEUM
Regular Admission: Adults $2.25, Children (7-12) 75¢
WITH THIS COUPON: Adults $1.25, Children 50¢
Valid until October 31, 1987

RAILROAD MUSEUM OF PENNSYLVANIA
Regular Admission: Adults $2.00, Children $1.00
WITH THIS COUPON: Adults $1.50
Valid during 1987

TENNESSEE VALLEY RAILROAD MUSEUM
Regular Fare: Adults $5.50, Children $3.00
WITH THIS COUPON: $1.00 off Adults & Children
(limit 1 per coupon)
Valid during 1987

OIL CREEK & TITUSVILLE RAILROAD
Regular Fare: Adults $7.00, Seniors $6.00 & Children $4.00
WITH THIS COUPON: 50¢ off Adults, Seniors & Children
Valid until September 31, 1987

CENTER FOR TRANSPORTATION & COMMERCE
Regular Admission: Adults $4.00, Sen. $3.00, Children $2.00
WITH THIS COUPON: 50¢ off Adults, Seniors & Children
Valid until March 31, 1988

"AGE OF STEAM" RAILROAD MUSEUM
Regular Admission: Adults $2.00, Children $1.00
WITH THIS COUPON: Adults $1.50, Children 75¢
Valid until June 1, 1988

GREEN MOUNTAIN RAILROAD
Regular Fare: Varies with trip
WITH THIS COUPON: $1.00 off any round trip ticket
(limit 2 per coupon)
Valid from June 20 to October 25, 1987

HEBER CREEPER SCENIC R.R.
Regular Fare: Adults $9.50, Children $5.00
WITH THIS COUPON: Adults $8.50, Children $4.50
Valid until October 11, 1987

STEAM PASSENGER DIRECTORY 1987 GUEST COUPONS

Savings for you and your family shown on reverse side of coupon

PUGET SOUND & SNOQUALMIE VALLEY R.R.
SNOQUALMIE, WASHINGTON
Steam Passenger Directory
1987 Guest Coupon

LAKE WHATCOM RAILWAY
WICKERSHAM, WASHINGTON
Steam Passenger Directory
1987 Guest Coupon

CASS SCENIC RAILROAD
CASS, WEST VIRGINIA
Steam Passenger Directory
1987 Guest Coupon

LAONA & NORTHERN RAILWAY
LAONA, WISCONSIN
Steam Passenger Directory
1987 Guest Coupon

MID-CONTINENT RAILWAY MUSEUM
NORTH FREEDOM, WISCONSIN
Steam Passenger Directory
1987 Guest Coupon

KETTLE MORAINE RAILWAY
NORTH LAKE, WISCONSIN
Steam Passenger Directory
1987 Guest Coupon

PARK LANE MODEL RAILROAD MUSEUM
REEDSBURG, WISCONSIN
Steam Passenger Directory
1987 Guest Coupon

HERITAGE PARK HISTORICAL VILLAGE
CALGARY, ALBERTA
Steam Passenger Directory
1987 Guest Coupon

SALEM & HILLSBOROUGH RAILROAD
HILLSBOROUGH, NEW BRUNSWICK
Steam Passenger Directory
1987 Guest Coupon

HALTON COUNTY RADIAL RAILWAY
ROCKWOOD, ONTARIO
Steam Passenger Directory
1987 Guest Coupon

1987 GUEST COUPON

Savings Available And Conditions For Use

LAKE WHATCOM RAILWAY
Regular Fare: Adults $6.00, Children $3.00
WITH THIS COUPON: Adults $5.00 on regularly
scheduled trains
(limit 2 per coupon)
Valid from June 6 to August 29, 1987

PUGET SOUND & SNOQUALMIE VALLEY R.R.
Regular Fare: Adults $5.00, Seniors $4.00 & Children $3.00
WITH THIS COUPON: $1.00 off regular fare
(limit 8 per coupon)
Valid until October 20, 1987

LAONA & NORTHERN RAILWAY
Regular Fare: Adults $8.00, Children $3.75 (plus tax)
WITH THIS COUPON: Adults $7.50 (plus tax)
Valid from June 22 to August 29, 1987

CASS SCENIC RAILROAD
Regular Fare: Varies with trip
WITH THIS COUPON: $1.00 off for Adults,
50¢ off for Children
Valid until November 1, 1987

KETTLE MORAINE RAILWAY
Regular Fare: Adults $5.00, Children $2.50 (plus tax)
WITH THIS COUPON: Adults $4.50, Children $2.25 (plus tax)
Valid from June 7 to October 18, 1987

MID-CONTINENT RAILWAY MUSEUM
Regular Fare: Adults $6.00, Children $3.00
WITH THIS COUPON: Adults $4.80, Children $2.40
Valid until September 27, 1987

HERITAGE PARK HISTORICAL VILLAGE
Train Ride: Adults, Children $1.00
WITH THIS COUPON: Adults & Children, Train Ride Free
Valid until September 7, 1987

PARK LANE MODEL RAILROAD MUSEUM
Regular Admission: Adults $3.00, Children $1.50
WITH THIS COUPON: Adults $2.00, Children $1.00
Valid until September 1987

HALTON COUNTY RADIAL RY.
Regular Fare: Adults $3.25, Seniors & Children $1.50
WITH THIS COUPON: 50¢ off Adults, Seniors & Children
Valid until October 25, 1987

SALEM & HILLSBOROUGH RAILROAD
Regular Fare: Adults $5.00, Children $2.25
WITH THIS COUPON: Adults $4.00, Children $2.00
Valid until September 7, 1987

WISCONSIN, EAST TROY
East Troy Electric Railroad
Wisconsin Trolley Museum

Electric, scheduled

Standard gauge

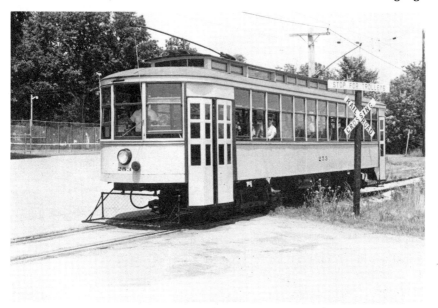

Photo by Scott Stankovsky

Location: East Troy is located about 30 miles southwest of Milwaukee. From Milwaukee, take Hwy. 15 to the Hwy. 20 exit, then turn west on Hwy. ES. The passenger station is at 2002 Church St. in East Troy.

Ride: A 10-mile, 1-hour trolley ride over original trackage of the famed Milwaukee Electric Railway & Light Co. This line was part of a vast network of electric interurban lines throughout southeastern Wisconsin and was originally built in 1907.

Schedule: Saturdays & Sundays, Memorial Day week-end through October. Cars leave East Troy at 11:30 A.M., 12:45, 2:00, 3:15 & 4:30 P.M. Also Wednesdays, Thursdays & Fridays, June 15 through August 20. Cars leave East Troy at 11:30 A.M., 12:45 & 2:00 P.M. Closed Holidays.

Fare: Adults $4.00, Children $2.00.

Trolleys: East Troy #100, ex-C.T.A. #4420; Duluth streetcar #253 (1914) and South Shore #11 & #30.

Displays: Electric cars on display include open car #21, South Shore #25, LaCrosse #56, Sheboygan Interurban #27 and LaCrosse Birney #12.

Paul J. Averdung, President

✔Refreshments
✔Gift Shop
✔Picnic Area
✔Memberships

East Troy Electric Railroad
P.O. Box 436
East Troy, WI 53120
Phone (414) 642-3263 (Operating Hours)
(414) 542-5573 (other times)

Location: Rail America is located at 2285 S. Broadway in Green Bay, one mile north of Highway 172, just off Business Route U.S. 41.

Schedule: Open Daily, May 1 through October 15 from 9:00 A.M. to 5:00 P.M.

Admission: Adults $4.00, Seniors $3.50, Children (6-12) $2.50, Family $14.00. Group rates available.

Displays: Rail America features one of the larger and more comprehensive collections of locomotives, passenger cars and freight equipment in the country. Of special interest are Winston Churchill's private cars and General Dwight D. Eisenhower's World War II staff train. Daily guided tours of passenger cars are offered.

Train: Included in the admission price is a ride aboard an 1890's passenger coach on a loop track through the grounds. Train operates at frequent intervals during each day.

Locomotives (Partial Listing): #101, 2-8-0, Baldwin (1917), ex-Korean Rys.; #261, 4-8-4, Alco (1944), ex-Milwaukee Road; #506, 2-10-2, Alco (1919), ex-D.M.&I.R.; #4017, 4-8-8-4, Alco (1941), ex-Union Pacific "Big Boy"; #5017, 2-10-4, Baldwin (1944), ex-Santa Fe; #60008, 4-6-2, Doncaster (1937), ex-British Railways.

Note: New exhibits have been built for the 1987 season, which celebrates the 125th anniversary of the first railroad to reach Green Bay, the Chicago & North Western.

Jerry Musich, Executive Director

✔Gift Shop
✔Picnic Area
✔Memberships

Rail America
The National Railroad Museum
2285 S. Broadway
Green Bay, WI 54304
Phone (414) 435-RAIL (Museum)
(414) 437-ROAD (Offices)

Location: The depot is located at Laona on Highways 8 and 32 in northern Wisconsin.

Ride: A 20-minute ride from Laona to Camp Five Farm attractions. The "Lumberjack Special" runs through scenic Wisconsin woodlands.

Schedule: Daily except Sundays, June 22 through August 29. Trains leave at 11:00 A.M., Noon, 1:00 & 2:00 P.M. Last train returns to Laona at 4:00 P.M. The train is operated by the Camp Five Museum Foundation, Inc., a non-profit foundation.

Fare: Adults $8.00, Children (3-12) $3.75, Maximum Family Rate for 2 Adults and 2 to 4 Children under 12, $21.50. Tax must be added to all tickets. Your ticket includes train ride and all attractions at Camp Five Farm except Hayrack and Pontoon Boat Trip. Group discounts for 30 or more.

Locomotives: #4, "The 4-Spot", 2-6-2, Vulcan (1916).

Train: Soo Line and Illinois Central steel coaches. Soo Line and D.M.&I.R. cabooses.

Displays: Logging museum, blacksmith shop, audio-visual, old-time country store, animal corral, forest tour by surrey and guides, ecology walk and 30-minute TV documentary "The Steam Engine". Extra fee: Hayrack and pontoon boat tour along wilderness bird refuge of the Rat River and wild rice banks. Adults $1.50, Children $1.00.

Mrs. Gordon R. Connor, Executive Director

✔Refreshments
✔Gift Shop
✔Picnic Area

Laona & Northern Ry.
Laona, WI 54541
Phone (715) 674-3620

Photo by R. M. Hinebaugh

Location: North Lake is located at the junction of Highways VV & 83, and is 20 miles northwest of Milwaukee. The site is 9 miles north of Interstate 94.

Ride: A leisurely, nostalgic 8-mile round trip over a former Milwaukee Road branchline. The train departs from the 1889 depot in North Lake, travels up 2% grades, through 2 moraine cuts and crosses the Oconomowoc River on a 125 ft. timber trestle. Real live steam, our heritage of the past for all ages, rain or shine.

Schedule: Steam train operates Sundays, from first Sunday in June through the third Sunday in October, plus Labor Day. Departs North Lake Depot at 1:00, 2:30 & 4:00 P.M. (C.D.T.).
Time subject to change to meet operating conditions when necessary. Extra train leaves at 11:00 A.M., Sundays in October for Autumn Color. Charter trips and group rates available.

Fare: Adults $5.00, Children (3-11) $2.50, under 3 free. Plus tax.

Locomotives: #9, 2-6-2, Baldwin (1901), ex-McCloud River R.R.

Train: Steel coaches, combination car, "hobo car", caboose.

Displays: #1000, ex-Chicago Great Western E.M.D. gas-electric car. #3, 0-4-0 gas-powered switcher, Davenport (1943). #3, 63-ton Heisler, ex-Craig Mountain R.R. (under restoration). Restored 1889 railroad depot at North Lake.

✔Refreshments
✔Gift Shop
✔Picnic Area

Mailing Address:
Kettle Moraine Railway
2430 Rockway Lane East
Brookfield, WI 53005
Phone (414) 782-8074
Depot Phone (414) 966-2866

WISCONSIN, NORTH FREEDOM
Mid-Continent Railway Museum

Steam, scheduled
Standard gauge

Location: The Museum is located 7 miles west of Baraboo, home of Circus World Museum. Follow Route 136 west to Road PF, then to North Freedom. The Museum is ½-mile west of the four corners.

Ride: This large, active volunteer group offers a 9-mile, 50-minute round trip over a former C.&N.W. branch line. An authentically restored steam train leaves from North Freedom where a large collection of rail equipment is displayed, runs to Quartzite Lake and return. The Museum has been at North Freedom since 1963.

Schedule: Steam trains operate Daily, May 11 thru Sept. 7. Also week-ends, Labor Day thru Oct. 18. Trains lv. at 10:30 A.M., 12:30, 2:00 & 3:30 P.M. Autumn Color trips 1st & 2nd week-ends of October. Snow Train, 3rd week-end of February. Send large SASE for free brochure.

Fare: Adults $6.00, Children $3.00, Family (2 Adults & 2 or more Children) $18.00. Group discounts available.

Locomotives: #9, 2-6-0, Baldwin (1884), ex-Dardanelle & Russellville.
#1, 4-6-0, Baldwin (1906), ex-Warren & Ouachita Valley Ry.
#1, 4-6-0, Montreal (1913), ex-Western Coal & Coke Co.
#2, 2-8-2, Baldwin (1912), ex-Saginaw Timber.
#440, 2-8-0, Baldwin (1902), ex-Union Pacific (under restoration).
#49, 2-8-0, Alco (1929), ex-Kewaunee, Green Bay & Western.
#31, Gas-electric car, EMC (1925), ex-Montana Western Ry.
#988, RSC-2 diesel, Alco (1947), ex-Milwaukee Road.

Train: Open-platform cars from the D.L.&W. R.R. used in regular operation. Wooden, open-vestibule coaches, combination car, restored to original appearance, used periodically.

Displays: Historically significant collection of locomotives, freight and passenger equipment, snowplows (including 1912 steam rotary), steam wreckers, 1894 C.&N.W. depot and operating wooden water tower. Artifact and photography exhibits in depot and coach shed.

Note: Locomotive #1385, Chicago & North Western 4-6-0, Alco (1907), may operate main-line trips this season. Call or write for details.

✔Refreshments
✔Gift Shop
✔Picnic Area
✔Memberships

Mid-Continent Railway Museum
P.O. Box 55
North Freedom, WI 53951
Phone (608) 522-4261

WISCONSIN, REEDSBURG
Park Lane Model Railroad Museum

Toy Train Museum

Location: The Museum is located in the Wisconsin Dells area near Exit 89 of Interstate 90 & 94. The building is at the intersection of State Route 23 and Herwig Road.

Displays: The Museum features a collection of over 2000 models on display. Trains shown are in every gauge and of all ages. There are several operating model railroad lay-outs which may be seen. Models range from tiny Z gauge through N, HO, S, O, Standard and Buddy L.

Schedule: Open Daily, rain or shine, Memorial Day through Labor Day, 10:00 A.M. to 6:00 P.M.

Admission: Adults $3.00, Children (6-12) $1.50, 5 and under free with paid Adult admission.

Note: Park Lane Model Railroad Museum is located 11 miles from the Circus World Museum in Baraboo and 14 miles from the Mid-Continent Railway Museum in North Freedom.

✔Gift Shop

Park Lane Model Railroad Museum
R.R. #1, Box 154A
Reedsburg, WI 53959

190

Location: Heritage Park is located on 66 acres of rolling parkland in southwest Calgary, at Heritage Drive and 14th Street S.W. With over 100 restored buildings and exhibits assembled from many parts of western Canada, the Park serves as an authentic living memorial to pre-1915 western settlement.

Rides: A visit begins with a 7-minute scenic trolley ride from the 14th St. entrance over a winding route to the Park's main gate. Inside the Park, a steam train operates continuously on a 20-minute schedule, using two 1885 open-platform coaches and ex-Canadian National mountain observation car "Mt. Resplendent".

Schedule: Daily, May 16 through September 7, then week-ends only to October 12, 1987.

Admission: To Park: Adults $4.50, Seniors & Students $3.25, Children $2.00. Train Ride: $1.00 per person.
Trolley: 25¢ per person each way between parking area and main gate.

Locomotives: #2023, 0-6-0, Alco (1942), ex-U.S. Army #4012. (Operating).
#2024, 0-6-0, Lima (1944), ex-U.S. Army #4076. (Operating).
#5934, 2-10-4, Montreal (1949), ex-Canadian Pacific #5931.
#4, 0-6-0, Angus Shops (1905), ex-Canadian Pacific #6144.

Trolleys: #14, double-truck closed car, Ottawa Car (1910), ex-Calgary Municipal.
#3, double-truck open observation, Montreal Tramways (1924).

Railroad Buildings: Original stations from Bowell, Laggan, Midnapore and Shepard. Water tank and sand tower. 6-stall roundhouse and single-track engine-shed.

Railroad Displays: Business Car #76 (1882), used at Last Spike Ceremonies on completion of C.P.R.R. Nov. 7, 1885; Private Car #100 (1901), ex-Dominion of Canada #100 (Prime Minister's Car); Business Car #5 (1902) "Pacific"; Canadian Pacific wooden colonist cars, coaches. Freight cars and work equipment.

Rick Smith, General Manager

✔Refreshments
✔Gift Shop
✔Picnic Area
✔Restaurant
✔Public Transportation

Heritage Park
1900 Heritage Drive S.W.
Calgary, Alberta T2V 2X3
Canada
Phone (403) 255-1182

CANADA, EDMONTON, ALBERTA
Alberta Pioneer Railway Assn.

Steam, Diesel, scheduled
Standard gauge

High Iron Photos

Location: The site of the Alberta Pioneer Ry. is at 24215 34th St., Edmonton. Take Highway 28 north to Namao, turn right at the brown highway sign and proceed east for 4¼ miles, then turn right and proceed south for 1 mile, Museum entrance is on the left before Zaychuk Nursery.

Ride: A 15-minute ride over a ⅓ mile stretch of trackage.

Schedule: Trains will operate on an expanded schedule for 1987. Steam loco #1392 will operate May 16-18, June 6-8, July 4-6 & 25-31, Aug. 1-3, Sept. 5-7, Oct. 10-11. Diesel #9000 will run July 11-12 & 18-19, Aug. 8-9, 15-16, 22-23 & 29-30, Oct. 12. Trains run Noon to 5:00 P.M. The site is open to visitors on Saturdays year-round and on Sundays, May 17 to Oct. 11, Noon to 5:00 P.M.

Fare: Adults $3.00, Seniors & Students $2.00, under 12 $1.00.

Locomotives: #73, 2-8-0, Canadian (1927), ex-Northern Alberta Rys.
#1392, 4-6-0, Montreal (1913), ex-Canadian National.
#6060, 4-8-2, Montreal (1944), ex-Canadian National.
#9000, 1500 h.p. Model F-3A diesel, E.M.D. (1948), ex-C.N.R.
#4104, C-liner diesel, Canadian (1954), ex-C.P.R.
#4459, Model F-7B diesel, G.M.D. (1953), ex-C.P.R.
#7944, Model NW-2 diesel, E.M.D. (1946), ex-C.N.R.

Train: Combination baggage car and coach. Diesel may be used as motive power in place of steam if necessary. Diesel will be used in switching before and after operations.

Displays: There are 55 pieces of freight and passenger rolling stock here including an Intercolonial Railway baggage car from 1877. Smaller artifacts may be seen in the former Canadian Northern Railway station of 1909.

✔Refreshments
✔Gift Shop
✔Memberships

Alberta Pioneer Railway Assn.
P.O. Box 6102, Station C
Edmonton, Alberta T5B 4K5
Canada

CANADA, EDMONTON, ALBERTA
Edmonton Radial Railway Society

Steam, Electric, scheduled
Standard gauge

Location: The Edmonton, Yukon & Pacific Ry. and the Edmonton Radial Railway Society are located within Fort Edmonton Park. The Park is located at Fox Drive and the south end of the Quesnell Bridge (Whitemud Freeway).

Ride: The steam train provides a 2-mile, 20-minute ride from the Park entrance to reconstructed Fort Edmonton. The streetcar line runs from the main entrance along streets of the 1905, 1920 and 1950 eras in Edmonton.

Schedule: Steam train and streetcars operate in conjunction with the Park's season. Daily, May 15 to September 7 from 10:00 A.M. to 6:00 P.M. Week-ends only, September 12 to October 12 from 1:00 to 5:00 P.M.

Admission: Train and streetcar rides included in admission to Park. Adults $4.00, Youths (13-17) $2.50, Children (6-12) $1.50, Seniors $2.00, Family $11.00.

Locomotives: #107, 2-6-2, Baldwin (1919), ex-Oakdale & Gulf Ry.

Trolleys: #1, Ottawa Car Co. (1908), #42, St. Louis Car Co. (1912), both cars ex-Edmonton Radial Railway Co.

Train: Combination coach #676 (1913), Day coach #304 (1914), open car, Canadian National caboose.

Displays: The Edmonton Radial Railway Society is in the process of restoring a number of old, original Edmonton cars. There is a 1908 streetcar barn, workshop and offices.

✔Refreshments
✔Gift Shop
✔Picnic Area
✔Memberships

Edmonton Radial Railway Society
3543 - 106A Street
Edmonton, Alberta T6J 1A7
Canada

Location: One Van Horne St. on Highway 3-95 in Cranbrook.

Displays: The Museum features the preserved and restored cars from the famous "Trans-Canada Limited" built by the Canadian Pacific Railway as their prestige train in 1929.

DINING CAR "ARGYLE" — contains restored inlaid black walnut panelling, Axminster carpet and valuable displays of original CPR furniture, china, glassware and silverware in the dining room. The dining room also serves light refreshments.

SOLARIUM LOUNGE CAR "RIVER ROUGE" — contains restored inlaid black walnut panelling, Axminster carpet and original furniture in the various parlours and the solarium.

BAGGAGE CAR — contains a complete exhibition gallery for changing art and history displays, reception and office use, plus gift shop.

SLEEPING CAR "RUTHERGLEN" — A sleeper containing 1 drawing room, 2 compartments and 8 upper and lower berth sections.

BUSINESS CAR "BRITISH COLUMBIA" — while not a part of the Trans-Canada Limited, it is a 1928 C.P.R. Business Car, completely original.

COMBINATION CAR #4489 — an original car which contains the museum's restoration/interpretation displays and slide show. The sleeping section was completely restored in 1987.

These beautiful cars are the last that remain from "Canada's Million-Dollar Train" and have been methodically restored to their original elegance.

Schedule: Mid-May thru early September, Daily, 9:00 A.M. - 8:00 P.M. Tea Room open daily. September through mid-May, Daily, Noon - 5:00 P.M. Tea Room, Sundays only.

Admission: Guided-tour of train, nominal charge.

Garry W. Anderson, Executive Director

✔Refreshments   The Railway Museum in Cranbrook
✔Gift Shop   Box 400
✔Memberships   Cranbrook, B.C. V1C 4H9, Canada
                                                           Phone (604) 489-3918

CANADA, DUNCAN, BRITISH COLUMBIA
British Columbia Forest Museum Park

Steam, scheduled
36" gauge

Location: The British Columbia Forest Museum Park is located on Vancouver Island, on Highway 1, about a mile north of Duncan and 55 minutes from Victoria.

Ride: A 1½-mile steam-powered narrow gauge railway. Train passes through forested areas and over a long curved wood trestle, passing logging camp and historic machinery.

Schedule: The Park is open May 2 through September 27, 1987. Steam train operates Daily, leaving every half-hour from 10:00 A.M. to 5:00 P.M. Locomotive #24 operates during May and June; #25 runs during July and August; Shay #1 operates on holiday weekends and special days. (Schedule subject to amendment).

Admission: Adults $3.95, O.A.P. $2.95, Students (6-16) $2.95, Family $10.00.
Special group rates available.

Locomotives: #1, 2-truck logging Shay, Lima (1921); #24, 0-4-0T, 12 ton Vulcan side tank (1900); #25, 0-4-0T, 18 ton Vulcan saddle tank; #22 gas locie, Plymouth (1926); #26, 10 ton Plymouth; #27, 8-wheeled logging crew speeder with trailer.

Train: Steel open platform coaches and open cars.

Displays: Standard gauge Shay and Climax locomotives, railroad logging equipment, including log cars and donkey engines. Log Museum on the site of the first community building in the Cowichan Valley, 1863. Logging camp with tours and films.

✔Picnic Area
✔Refreshments

British Columbia Forest Museum Park
Trans Canada Highway, R.R. #4
Duncan, B.C. V9L 3W8, Canada
Phone (604) 746-1251

CANADA, FORT STEELE, BRITISH COLUMBIA
East Kootenay Railway

Steam, scheduled
Standard gauge

Location: The East Kootenay Railway operates in Fort Steele Heritage Park in eastern British Columbia. Fort Steele is located near Cranbrook on Routes 93-95 and is on the main-line of the Canadian Pacific Ry.

Ride: Passengers enjoy a 2.3 mile, 25-minute ride through the grounds of the park. The double-loop track climbs to the Kootenay River Lookout, where riders disembark to enjoy the majestic scenery. The Conductor gives a brief talk on local history and railroading before the train returns to the station.

Schedule: Steam train operates on week-ends from May 16 to June 22, then Daily operation from June 26 to September 7, 1987. Train makes regular departures from 10:00 A.M. to 5:00 P.M. Train leaves from the period Canadian Pacific Railway shed-roof station at Fort Steele.

Fare: Adults $3.50, Children $1.50, under 6 free.

Locomotives: #115, "Robert E. Swanson", 3-truck Pacific Coast Shay, Lima (1934). "Dunrobin", 0-4-4T, Sharp, Stewart (1895), built for the Duke of Sutherland in Scotland.

Train: British Railways coach and open-air car with benches.

Displays: Railroad displays include an ex-CPR snowplow and caboose and the Highland Railway private railway carriage belonging with the "Dunrobin".

✔Refreshments
✔Gift Shop
✔Picnic Area
✔Free Parking

East Kootenay Railway Co.
Fort Steele, B.C. V0B 1N0
Phone (604) 489-3229

CANADA, NORTH VANCOUVER, B.C.
Royal Hudson Steam Train

Steam, scheduled
Standard gauge

Location: Train departs from the BC Rail station at the foot of Pemberton St. in North Vancouver.

Ride: A spectacular 40-mile trip to Squamish and return. The total ride is 80 miles and takes 5½-hours, including a 1 hr.-40 min. stopover at Squamish. The highly scenic trip operates along the coast of Howe Sound, with the island dotted sea on one side of the train and the coastal mountains on the other side. Combination rail/boat trip is also offered, in either direction.

Schedule: Wednesdays through Sundays from May 17 through September 27, plus Monday, August 3. Boarding begins at 9:00 A.M. and all seating is on a first come-first served basis. Train departs North Vancouver 10:30 A.M., arrives Squamish 12:20 P.M. Leaves Squamish 2:00 P.M., arrives North Vancouver 3:55 P.M.

Fare: Adults $20.00; Seniors & Students (12-18) $16.00; Children (5-11) $12.00, under 5 free. Reservations required.

Locomotives: #2860, 4-6-4, Montreal (1940), ex-Canadian Pacific Ry. This locomotive is a stainless-steel jacketed "Royal Hudson" type. Resplendent in polished maroon and black, this engine makes a fine sight at the head of its matching maroon passenger train.

Train: Baggage car, coaches, club cars.

Railroad: Passenger train operates over the main-line of BC Rail, a 1000+ mile freight railroad. BC Rail also offers scheduled passenger trains, composed of Budd RDC cars, from North Vancouver to Lillooet and Prince George, B.C.

Note: Steam train reservations may be made by telephone, using Visa, MasterCard or Amex credit cards.

✔Refreshments on train
✔Gift Shop
✔Picnic Area
✔Free Parking

Royal Hudson Steam Train Society
744 West Hastings St. Suite 206
Vancouver, B.C. V6C 1A5, Canada
Phone (604) 68-TRAIN or
(604) 687-9558

CANADA, WINNIPEG, MANITOBA
Prairie Dog Central

Steam, scheduled
Standard gauge

Photo by D. Shores

Location: Train departs from the C.N. St. James Station located nearby to 1661 Portage Ave. just west of St. James St. Courtesy parking.

Ride: A 36-mile, 2-hour round trip to Grosse Isle over the Oakpoint Subdivision of the Canadian National Railways. Vintage wooden cars are pulled by a beautiful American Standard type locomotive which was in active service on the Canadian Pacific from 1882 to 1918.

Schedule: Sundays only, June through September. Trains leave Winnipeg 11:30 A.M. and 3:00 P.M. Central Daylight Saving Time.

Fare: Adults $8.00, Seniors & Students (12-17) $5.00, Children (3-11) $4.00, under 3 - free on knee. Fares slightly higher during July & August.

Locomotives: #3, 4-4-0, Dubs & Co., Glasgow, Scotland (April 1882). This locomotive was sold to the City of Winnipeg Hydro by the Canadian Pacific in 1918 and used by them until 1962. Vintage Locomotive Society operates and maintains the engine under a lease agreement with the City of Winnipeg. The Centennial for Locomotive #3 was 1982.

Train: Wood combination car, four wood coaches and one steel coach. Steel coach used during July and August.

Displays: On display in the City of Winnipeg are Canadian National locomotives #2747, a 2-8-0 and #6043, a 4-8-2.

✔Refreshments
✔Gift Shop
✔Memberships

The Vintage Locomotive Society, Inc.
Box 217, St. James P.O.
Winnipeg, Manitoba
R3J 3R4 Canada
Phone (204) 284-2690

Photo by James L. O'Donnell

Location: Route 114 in Hillsborough, 14 miles (24 km) south of Moncton.

Ride: A 10-mile, 1-hour round trip between Hillsborough and Salem. Train crosses 44 ft. high wooden trestle. A number of curves make for excellent picture taking from the train. Fall Foliage and Dinner trips continue past Salem to Baltimore making a 22 mile round trip.

Schedule:

June 26-Sept. 7: Daily	1:30 3:00 4:30 P.M.
May 16-June 21: Week-ends	1:30 3:00
Sept. 12-Sept. 27: Week-ends	1:30 3:00
Oct. 3-Oct. 31: Week-ends	2:15 (3 hr. Fall Foliage)
Dec. 27-Dec. 31: Daily	1:30 (Snow Trains)

Fare: Regular trains: Adults $5.00, Seniors $4.50, Children (6-12) $2.50, under 6 free. Family $15.00.

Locomotives: #42, 2-6-0, Schenectady (1899), ex-Sydney & Louisburg Ry.
#1009, 4-6-0, Montreal (1912), ex-Canadian National Rys.
#8208, RS-1 diesel, Alco (1946), ex-Cape Breton Development.
#7941, NW-2 diesel, E.M.D. (1946), ex-Canadian National Rys.

Train: Open-air cars, CNR steel coaches, 1911 Pullman sleeper.

Dining Train: "The SUNSET" offers great food during a 3½-hour trip between Hillsborough and Baltimore. Diesel #8208 pulls a Dining car, 2 Lounge Cars and "Le Bistro" entertainment coach. Operates Wednesday thru Saturday during July & August and Week-ends in June, September & October. Late afternoon departures vary with season. Reservations required.

Displays: #29, 4-4-0, CPR Shops (1887), ex-Canadian Pacific Ry. Also a double-ended snowplow, wooden cabooses, CPR 100-ton steam wrecker and numerous CNR and CPR passenger and freight cars.

Note: September 5-6, 1987, 100th birthday party for CPR #29. Double-headed trains and special events each day.

✔Refreshments
✔Gift Shop
✔Picnic Area
✔Snack Bar
✔Dining Car
✔Memberships

TRAIN

Salem & Hillsborough Railroad
P.O. Box 70
Hillsborough, N.B. E0A 1X0
Canada
Phone (506) 734-3195
(800) 332-3989 (within New Brunswick)

*The Museum's operating steam train on its 1986 trip to Expo '86
in Vancouver, British Columbia.*

Location: The Museum is located on a 35-acre site at 1867 St. Laurent Blvd. in southeast Ottawa.

Displays: This excellent science museum features all types of transportation, from Canada's earliest days to the present time. There are also many other types of exhibits relating to science and technology.

There are 9 steam locomotives on display, many in huge Railroad Hall. This large room contains 7 locomotives, some of which allow access to the cabs, where sound effects give the feeling of live locomotives. The engines are meticulously restored, with polished rods and with lighted number boards and class lights. The scene is enhanced by station benches, platform lights, signs and displays of memorabilia.

Locomotives: Canadian National engines include #5700, 4-6-4, Montreal (1930); #6400, 4-8-4, Montreal (1936), displayed at 1939 N.Y. World's Fair. Canadian Pacific engines include #926, 4-6-0, (1911); #2858, 4-6-4, Royal Hudson, Montreal (1938); #3100, 4-8-4, Montreal (1928). Also, CNR #40, 4-4-0, Portland (1872) and CNR #247, 0-6-0T with 2 coaches, circa 1890. CNR narrow-gauge passenger car from Newfoundland.

Schedule: Open Daily, May 1-September 7 from 10:00 A.M. to 8:00 P.M. Balance of year, open Daily 9:00 A.M. to 5:00 P.M. Closed on Mondays during Winter except Holiday Mondays. Closed Christmas Day.

Admission: No Charge.

Note: The Museum's steam excursion trips will not operate on a regular basis in 1987. Contact the Museum for information on any special trips that may be run.

✔Refreshments
✔Gift Shop
✔Free Parking

National Museum of Science & Technology
1867 St. Laurent Blvd.
Ottawa, Ontario K1A 0M8
Phone (613) 998-4566

CANADA, PORT STANLEY, ONTARIO
Port Stanley Terminal Rail

Diesel, scheduled
Standard gauge

Photo by Brad Jolliffe

Location: Port Stanley is located on Highway 4, south of London, Ont. It is about 20 minutes from Hwy. 401. Port Stanley is a small resort area on the shores of Lake Erie.

Ride: A trip from Port Stanley to Union over a portion of the former London & Port Stanley Ry. Two bridges are crossed as the train passes through fields and apple orchards. The 6-mile round trip takes 50 minutes.

Schedule: Trains depart from Port Stanley station (adjacent to lift bridge). Operate Saturdays, Sundays & Canadian Holidays, May through December. Depart hourly, 1:00 to 5:00 P.M. During July and August, trains also operate Wednesdays, Thursdays and Fridays at 1:00. 2:00 & 3:00 P.M.

Fare: Adults $4.00, Children $2.00, under 2 free.

Locomotives: L-1, 25-ton diesel, General Electric (1952).
L-2, 50-ton diesel, Whitcomb, Canadian Loco. Co. (1950).
Both locomotives, ex-Consolidated Sand & Gravel Co., Paris, Ont.
L-3, SW-9 diesel, G.M.D. (1951), ex-C.&O. #5242.

Train: Open excursion cars, ex-T.H.&B. coach/caboose #66.

Displays: Canadian Pacific business car #24 (1929), restored ex-Canadian National caboose #78491, T.H.&B. caboose #61, ex-C.&O. burro crane #6. Ticket office, gift shop and displays contained in ex-London & Port Stanley station.

✓Refreshments
✓Gift Shop
✓Memberships

Port Stanley Terminal Rail
P.O. Box 549
Port Stanley, Ont. N0L 2A0
Phone (519) 782-9993

Location: Take Highway 401 to Exit 312, Guelph Line. Travel north on Guelph Line 9 miles to reach the Museum site.

Ride: Located on the right-of-way of the old Toronto Suburban Ry., Canada's first operating railway museum offers a 2-mile ride through scenic woodlands. Two newly completed loops are now in service.

Schedule: Open from May 9 thru October 25, 1987. Cars operate Saturdays, Sundays & Holidays, May 9 thru October 25. Daily (except Monday & Tuesday) June 3-June 28, every day from July 1-September 7. Hours are 11:00 A.M. to 5:00 P.M. Trolley Extravaganzas, June 28 & September 27. Christmas Fiesta, December 6.

Fare: Adults $3.25, Seniors & Children $1.50, Students (13-17) $2.00, Family Rate $9.25. Special Days, extra fare. Group rates, charters, available.

Trolleys: #327, 4-wheel open car, T.T.C. (1893, rebuilt 1933). #55, single-truck closed car, Preston (1915). #2890, small Peter Witt, Ottawa (1923). Above cars ex-Toronto Transportation Commission. #8, heavy interurban car, Jewett Car Co. (1915), ex-London & Port Stanley Ry. #732, trolley coach, ex-Hamilton Street Rys.

Displays: Numerous pieces of electric railway rolling stock from lines in Canada, ranging from early wooden cars to P.C.C. cars from Toronto. Also on display are a line car, a crane car, sweeper, an electric locomotive, caboose and box cars.

Mrs. Joan Johns, Curator

✔Refreshments
✔Gift Shop
✔Picnic Area
✔Memberships

Ontario Electric Ry. Hist. Assn.
Box 121, Station "A"
Scarborough, Ont. M1K 5B9, Canada
Phone (519) 856-9802
when Museum is open.

CANADA, SAULT STE. MARIE, ONTARIO
Algoma Central Ry.

Diesel, scheduled
Standard gauge

Soo Photo Service Ltd.

Location: The Algoma Central is a common-carrier railroad which operates a 296 mile main-line from Sault Ste. Marie to Hearst, Ontario. The Algoma Central crosses the transcontinental main-lines of both the Canadian Pacific and Canadian National Rys.

Ride: The line traverses vast expanses of virtually untouched countryside, through forests and mountains, past countless lakes and rivers and through miles of northern muskeg. Spectacular Agawa Canyon is an awe-inspiring sight as the train cuts through a narrow defile in the mountains. The trip to the end of steel at Hearst requires an over-night stay in that French-Canadian town. One day Wilderness Tours are offered as well as the famous one day Snow Train. The Wilderness Tour runs to Agawa Canyon and return, while the Snow Train operates a few miles further north.

Schedule: To Hearst: Jan. 1-May 22 and Oct. 20-Dec. 31, train leaves Sault Ste. Marie on Fri., Sat. & Sun. Daily (except Monday) service, May 23 to Oct. 19. One Day Wilderness Tour operates Daily, June 8 to Oct. 18, 1987. Lv. Sault Ste. Marie 8:00 A.M., return 5:00 P.M., includes 2-hr. stopover at Agawa Canyon. Advance reservations not accepted, but tickets may be purchased at depot one day in advance of trip.
The Snow Train operates Saturdays & Sundays, January thru March. Lvs. S.S.M. 8:30 A.M., return 4:30 P.M. Due to low temperatures and heavy snow, there is no stopover. Reservations urgently recommended.

Fare: Write for complete timetables and schedule of fares.

Locomotives: The Algoma Central operates a fleet of modern diesel-electric locomotives painted a distinctive maroon and gray color.

Note: During the fall-color season, mid-September to mid-October, capacity crowds are experienced on week-ends. Try to plan your trip for a weekday if possible.

✔Refreshments on train
✔Gift Shop

Passenger Sales
Algoma Central Railway
P.O. Box 7000
Sault Ste. Marie, Ontario
P6A 1W7 Canada
Phone (705) 254-4331

Photo by Vaughn Butler

Location: The Museum is situated on a 70 acre site in the towns of Delson and St. Constant, 30 minutes from downtown Montreal. The entrance is located at 122a St. Pierre St. (Route 209), 1 mile south of the junction with Route 132.

Displays: The largest railway museum in Canada, the collection consists of over 100 examples of steam and diesel locomotives, passenger cars, freight cars, streetcars and interurbans. The collection traces the evolution of Canada's railways from the 19th century to the present. The Museum is a project of the Canadian Railroad Historical Assn. Guided tours for groups of 10 or more are available by advance reservation.

Schedule: Open Daily, May 2 through October 18 from 9:00 A.M. to 5:00 P.M.

Operation: A 1½-mile, 20-minute ride through the Museum grounds at no additional charge.
Streetcar operates Daily. Train operates Sundays & Holidays. Steam locomotive "John Molson" operates Sundays of Canadian Holiday week-ends.

Admission: Adults $3.50, Students $2.50, Pensioners (65+) $2.50, Children $1.75.

Train: Ex-C.N.R. self-propelled railcar #15824; ex-C.N.R. 70-ton G.E. diesel #30; T.S. Ry. open streetcar #8; steam locomotive "John Molson", 2-2-2 operating replica of 1850's engine.

✔Refreshments
✔Gift Shop
✔Picnic Area
✔Memberships

Canadian Railway Museum
P.O. Box 148
St. Constant, Quebec J0L 1X0
Phone (514) 632-2410

EMPIRE STATE
RAILWAY MUSEUM, INC.

Preserving Railroad History for New York and the Nation

E.S.R.M.'s locomotive #23, Lake Superior & Ishpeming R.R. 2-8-0, shown above, is now at Kingston, N.Y. along with a number of passenger cars.

The Museum is presently restoring the former Ulster & Delaware R.R. station at Phoenicia, N.Y.

Associate Memberships in the Museum available.

Active	$15	Donor	$25
Contributing	50	Patron	100
Life	500	Corporate	100 or more

For membership information, write:

EMPIRE STATE RAILWAY MUSEUM, INC.
Phoenicia Depot
P.O. Box 455
Phoenicia, N.Y. 12464

VOLUNTEERS NEEDED!

Mississippi Railway Museum

Photo by Louis Saillard

The *MISSISSIPPI RAILWAY MUSEUM*, formerly at Port Bienville, has now moved its operation to Meridian, Miss. The train is based at the Gulf, Mobile & Ohio Depot in Meridian. For information on schedule, route and fares, please send a large SASE to Mississippi Railway Museum, P.O. Box 15485, Hattiesburg, MS 39404.

TRA I N

SERVING CREATIVE RAILROADING

Our member organizations and individuals share two basic qualities: they are all leaders in the growing industry of creative railroading, and they are all Tourist Railway Association members. **TRAIN** is the one trade association that is serving the growing needs of tourist rail lines, railroad museums, excursion operators, private car owners and suppliers — the multi-faceted groups that make up creative railroading.

With over 200 members, and growing every month, our Roster is too long to print. Our members included in the STEAM PASSENGER DIRECTORY may be identified by the **TRAIN** logo on their listing page.

TRAIN members receive our bi-monthly magazine TRAINLINE, filled with articles relating to the tourist railway industry.

Each year, **TRAIN** holds an Annual Convention at a prominent railroad location. This year's meet will be hosted by the Mad River & NKP Railroad Society at Sandusky, Ohio on November 6, 7 & 8, 1987. For information on this event, write to the Convention Chairman, Bill Fuehring at Mad River & NKP R.R. Soc., P.O. Box 42, Bellevue, OH 44811 or call (419) 483-2222.

TRAIN is an action association, dealing decisively in the areas of *Legislation, *Safety, *Insurance, *Operations, *Mechanical-steam, *Mechanical-diesel, *Mechanical-electric, *Mechanical-passenger cars, *Advertising and *Promotion. For further information on this important alliance of professionals write:

The Tourist Railway Association, Inc., c/o Mrs. Judy Sandberg, 3315 Skyview Drive, Burnsville, Minnesota 55337.

TRAIN members: professionals in creative railroading

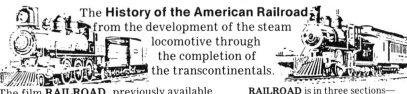

ASSOCIATION OF RAILWAY MUSEUMS, INC.
P.O. Box 3311
City of Industry, CA 91744-0311
Telephone: (818) 814-1438

"Promoting the Railway Museum Movement"

The professional society for organizations which have the common goal of preserving our railway heritage through acquisition, rehabilitation, restoration, operation, protection, and display of historic railway equipment.

MEMBERS

Alberta Pioneer Railway Assn.
Baltimore Streetcar Museum
Bay Area Electric Railroad Assn.
Boothbay Railway Village
Gerald E. Brookins Museum
Buckingham Valley Trolley Assn.
Center for Transport. & Commerce
Colorado Railroad Museum
Connecticut Valley RR Museum
Connecticut Electric Ry. Assn.
Conway Scenic Railroad
East Troy Electric Railroad
Edmonton Radial Railway Society
Florida Gulf Coast R. R. Museum
Fort Collins Municipal Ry. Society
Fort Smith Streetcar Rest. Assn.
Fox River Trolley Museum
Illinois Railway Museum
Indiana Railway Museum
Kentucky Railway Museum
Mad River & NKP Railroad Society
McKinney Avenue Transit Authority
Michigan Transit Museum
Midwest Electric Railway Assn.

Minnesota Transportation Museum
National Capital Trolley Museum
Northern Ohio Railway Museum
Ohio Railway Museum
Okefenoke Heritage Center
Ontario Electric Ry. Hist. Assn.
Orange Empire Railway Museum
Oregon Electric Ry. Hist. Society
Pacific Southwest Ry. Hist. Assn.
Pennsylvania Ry. Museum Assn.
Puget Sound Railway Hist. Assn.
Rail America
Railways To Yesterday
San Antonio Museum Assn.
San Jose Trolley Corporation
Seashore Trolley Museum
Smoky Hill Ry. & Hist. Society
Southwest Missouri Elec. Ry. Assn.
St. Louis & Chain Of Rocks R. R.
Tennessee Valley Railroad Museum
The Shore Line Trolley Museum
The Trolley Museum Of New York
Toronto and York Div. C.R.H.A.
Virginia Transportation Museum

Let us represent YOUR museum
Est. 1961
A Professional Affiliate Member of
the American Association of Museums

1987 Convention: Riverside, Calif.
October 15-19, 1987

For Convention Information write:
A.R.M. Convention Committee
P.O. Box 2858
Riverside, CA 92516-2858

Park Lane Model Railroad Museum

TRAINS RUN EVERY DAY.....RAIN OR SHINE

Displays of models that were built, painted, decaled and detailed by experts

OPERATING LAYOUTS
Plus Layout Under Construction

OPEN MEMORIAL DAY
THRU LABOR DAY

Hours:
Open Daily, rain or shine
10 AM to 6 PM

ADMISSION:

ADULTS - $3.00
CHILDREN (age 6 thru 12) $1.50
CHILDREN age 5 and under free.

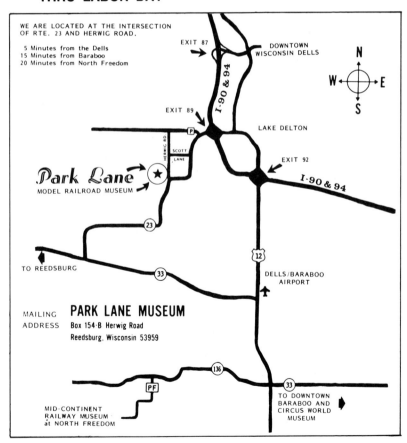

WE ARE LOCATED AT THE INTERSECTION
OF RTE. 23 AND HERWIG ROAD.

5 Minutes from the Dells
15 Minutes from Baraboo
20 Minutes from North Freedom

EXIT 87

DOWNTOWN
WISCONSIN DELLS

I-90 & 94

N
W — E
S

EXIT 89

P

LAKE DELTON

Park Lane
MODEL RAILROAD MUSEUM

★

HERWIG RD.

SCOTT
LANE

EXIT 92

I-90 & 94

23

TO REEDSBURG

33

12

DELLS/BARABOO
AIRPORT

MAILING
ADDRESS

PARK LANE MUSEUM
Box 154-B Herwig Road
Reedsburg, Wisconsin 53959

136

PF

MID-CONTINENT
RAILWAY MUSEUM
at NORTH FREEDOM

33

TO DOWNTOWN
BARABOO AND
CIRCUS WORLD
MUSEUM

are you a railroad enthusiast?
get on the right track by joining the RRE

THE RAILROAD ENTHUSIASTS, INC.

The RRE's 1600 members in eleven divisions across the country will tell you the RRE is the organization that's doing things. Back in 1934, the RRE was the first group to run railfan excursions. Fifty years later, it is still in the forefront with numerous trips each year, ranging from large scale main-line excursions to shortline mini-trips, shop tours and Dinner-in-the-Diner trips.

The divisions offer regular meetings with an extensive variety of railroad related entertainment — slides, movies, speakers, contests, etc. In addition to the fine "RRE Journal" (a comprehensive newsletter published ten times a year), each division publishes its own newsletter packed with coming events, local and regional news, special articles and news of members activities.

Each year, RRE has three national get-togethers — a workshop at Hartford, Connecticut, the end of January; a spring (or mid-year) meeting and an annual meeting in the fall. The location and programs for the last two meetings vary from year to year. However, they always include at least one trip, and generally a banquet and other entertainment.

For information on division and/or trip activities or membership, contact:

PORTLAND DIVISION, P.O. Box 641, Portland, ME 04104
LAKE REGION DIVISION, c/o David Collinge, 77 Horne St., Dover, NH 03820
MASSACHUSETTS BAY DIVISION, P.O. Box 136, Ward Hill, MA 01830
HARTFORD DIVISION, c/o Paul Yurko, 14 Westgate Cir., Newington, CT 06111
NEW YORK DIVISION, P.O. Box 1318, Grand Central Sta., New York, NY 10017
CHESAPEAKE DIVISION, P.O. Box 548, Laurel, MD 20707
OLD DOMINION DIVISION, c/o J.A. Tillman, 8708 Thunderbird Court, Vienna, VA 22180
FOREST CITY DIVISION, c/o J.A. Swift, 24101 Lake Shore Blvd., #312A, Euclid, OH 44123
QUEEN CITY DIVISION, c/o Gregory Molloy, 634 Flagstaff Dr., Cincinnati, OH 45215
ST. LOUIS DIVISION, c/o David A. Young, P.O. Box 1183, Maryland Hts., MO 63043

Groups or organizations interested in affiliation may contact:

David R. Squires, President - RRE, 7505 June St., Springfield, VA 22150

The RRE puts you where the action is . . .

The Depot Ltd. of Sullivan

PHONE 1-800-223-3768

IL & AK RESIDENTS
PLEASE CALL COLLECT
1-217-797-6351

OshKosh B'Gosh
CAPS
and
Overalls

Caps .....$5.00 ea.
Bandanas.$1.50 ea.

Overalls ....Full Range of Sizes
6/9 month......................15.95
Toddlers(12 mo.-24 mo.).....16.95
Boys'(2 yr,-12 yr,)...........16.95
Men's(13-50).................25.50

THE CANNONBALL
One Of The Most Exciting Watches To
Ever Come Down The Line

Available
in Men's &
Ladies Sizes
$49.95

The Perfect Gift For Railroaders
of All Ages. Hop aboard the Cannonball
and let your imagination ride this miniature train to a Journey to
Anywhere.
The gold and black locomotive chugs
around the track once a
minute........
The watches are 17 jewel, full lever,
shock resistant, anti- magnetic and
have a full year's guarantee.
Gold plated case; Gold expanded
band; Gift boxed.

THE DEPOT
Antique China   General Line
ANTIQUES & GIFTS
Glass-ware

West on Eden Street Road
SULLIVAN, ILLINOIS 61951

Use Your
VISA or MASTER CARD

We will be happy to accept your personal check or your
☐ Mastercard, ☐ VISA

Expiration Date   Credit Card Signature Required

THE GENERAL

AUTHENTIC TRAIN WHISTLE SOUND
FROM THE DAYS OF STEAM

**Cannonball Whistle Recreates
The Authentic Five Chime Steam
Engine Sound.**

Beautifully polished
all-aluminum train
whistle will take you on
a trip to yesteryear
when the steam engine
train was king. 9 ½"
long. Weighs just three ounces.
Makes an excellent gift for railroaders
of all ages. Includes instructions on
how to simulate train hiss and other
train sounds.

ALL ALUMINUM WHISTLE .$22.50
ALL BRASS WHISTLE......$57.50

CHECK THE DEPOT FOR A WIDE
VARIETY OF ITEMS
CONTENTS OF CATALOG

* Wrist Watches
* Pocket Watch
* Magic Mugs
* Train Whistle
* Buckles
* Belts
* Clocks
* Cassettes
* OshKosh Clothes
* Rug Beaters
* Phones
* Hobo Book
* Cast Iron Pot

* Farm & Plantation Bell
* Black Lab Doorstop
* Bulldog & Bank Doorstop
* Train Print (Framed)
* Commemorative Plate
* Lawn Sweep
* Horse Head
* Utility Cart

ORDER YOUR **FREE** CATALOG
TODAY!

Name Of Item	Size	Quan.	Price Each	Total Price
		SUBTOTAL		
IL RES. ADD 6.25% TAX				
		SHIPPING		
TOTAL AMT. ENCLOSED				

INDEX OF LISTINGS